1 MONTH OF
FREE
READING

at
www.ForgottenBooks.com

By purchasing this book you are eligible for one month membership to ForgottenBooks.com, giving you unlimited access to our entire collection of over 1,000,000 titles via our web site and mobile apps.

To claim your free month visit:
www.forgottenbooks.com/free268704

ISBN 978-0-428-19513-7
PIBN 10268704

FORTIFICATIONS APPROPRIATION BILL, 1921.

THURSDAY, APRIL 22, 1920.

UNITED STATES SENATE,
SUBCOMMITTEE OF COMMITTEE ON APPROPRIATIONS,
Washington, D. C.
The subcommittee met, pursuant to notice, at 10 o'clock a. m., Senator Reed Smoot presiding.
Present: Senators Smoot (chairman), Overman, and Harris.

STATEMENT OF HON. FREDERICK W. DALLINGER, A REPRESENTATIVE FROM THE STATE OF MASSACHUSETTS.

Senator SMOOT. You may proceed, Representative Dallinger.

Mr. DALLINGER. In the House, Representative Hull of Iowa and myself offered amendments to the first paragraph under "armament and fortifications" (p. 4, line 18), to increase the amount from $1,500,000 to $7,500,000; and on page 5, in the first paragraph under that same heading, increasing that amount from $2,000,000 to $3,900,000.

Senator SMOOT. Was there an estimate for these increases?

Mr. DALLINGER. I will state that I got the figures from the Ordnance Department, and the basis of increase in appropriations over the amount reported by the House Committee on Appropriations was what was absolutely essential to maintain a skeleton organization in the Army.

Senator SMOOT. What I wanted to know was, was there an estimate made for these increases?

Mr. DALLINGER. There was an estimate made from the Army.

Senator SMOOT. I mean from the Secretary of the Treasury?

Mr. DALLINGER. They asked for a great deal more than that. I understand Gen. Williams asked for a great deal more than that, but these figures represented the amount absolutely essential to maintain a skeleton organization.

Now, Mr. Chairman, this is not because there is any desire on my part to keep any men on the pay roll unnecessarily.

The Watertown Arsenal happens to be in my district, and, of course, there has got to be a very great further reduction in the force of employees in that arsenal. Everybody realizes that. During the war there were five or six thousand employees there. At present there are about 3,300, and in order to get back to a peace basis there will have to be a still further reduction.

All that I am interested in is to see the efficiency of the Military Establishment maintained. My position is this: Either the United States Government and Congress must assume that there is never going to be another war, and do away with the War Department and Navy Department, and ought to sell these arsenals, in which the people have invested hundreds of millions of dollars in land, buildings, and equipment, and realize upon them and turn the money back into the Treasury and save the expense of maintenance, or else they ought to maintain those arsenals by maintaining a skeleton organization sufficient to carry on experimental work, so that the lessons of this Great War may not be lost, and to have the different kinds of munitions manufactured, so that the art of making these things and keeping the manufacture up to date may not be lost, and in order that there may be maintained at Watertown, as was planned and as is being done so far as can be done now, a school for ordnance officers.

If we are ever going to have any war in the future, or if we want to be prepared for emergencies, it is essential that there should be trained in the Ordnance Department officers who are capable of manufacturing munitions of war in Government arsenals and in private plants.

There is no doubt whatever that we were unprepared in that respect at the outbreak of the late war, and in my opinion a tremendous saving could have been made if we had had the proper kind of training carried on to a sufficient extent to have trained a corps of Ordnance officers in sufficient numbers to have done this important work.

Now, of course you can not maintain a school for training Ordnance officers unless you have a plant to run, in the different parts, to some extent, and you can not carry on experimental work and keep the art of manufacturing these different kinds of ordnance up to date unless you carry on the manufacture to some extent.

Now, Col. Dickson, who was a brigadier general during the war and is now, as the result of the demobilization of the Army, a colonel, the commandant at the Watertown Arsenal, was asked to make an estimate of the smallest number of employees at that arsenal that would be sufficient to maintain a skeleton organization, and he estimated about 1,800. I understand that the Ordnance Bureau here revised those figures and thought that they could maintain a skeleton organization with a force of 1,375.

Gen. LORD. That is correct.

Mr. DALLINGER. And it was on that revised estimate that the figures which we offered in the House were based.

Now, so far as I can find out, what happened in the House committee was this: The estimates of the War Department were $118,-000,000 for this bill, if I recall correctly.

The House bill as reported was about $18,000,000, and as nearly as I can find out, carrying out the platform of economy as a political matter, a slash was made of $100,000,000. Of course, it is good politics. We have got to reduce because of the tremendous burden of taxation, and they were told, "you have got to reduce this bill $100,000,000." So the bill was arbitrarily reduced from $118,000,000 to $18,000,000.

Now, Mr. Chairman, it appears to me that that is not a scientific way of getting at the thing, and all we tried to do in the House was to raise that amount to about $26,000,000.

As I said on the floor of the House at the time the matter was up, if they were simply trying to reduce expenditures and reduce taxation, and were going to cripple the Military Establishment and make it impossible to maintain an efficient school for ordnance officers and to carry on this necessary experimental work and to do what ought to be done, the thing to do was to bring in no bill at all, to wipe out the whole $18,000,000, and sell these arsenals and realize the money and put it into the Treasury. In other words, there is a point below which you can not go; and so far as I am concerned this is a question of reducing the estimates from $118,000,000 to $26,000,000 instead of $18,000,000, as the House has done.

Senator OVERMAN. Are you a member of the House Committee on Appropriations?

Mr. DALLINGER. No, sir. I am interested in this matter because the Watertown arsenal is in my district.

Senator SMOOT. Do you know anything about the amount of the balances on hand for the purpose of ordnance and fortifications?

Mr. DALLINGER. No, sir. I understand the House bill provides for turning that all back into the Treasury—over $800,000,000.

Senator SMOOT. No; I mean for this item alone.

Mr. DALLINGER. Not for this item alone; but for all the items.

Senator OVERMAN. Was there any attempt made on the floor of the House to increase this amount?

Mr. DALLINGER. Yes; we made an attempt on the floor of the House, but, as you know, Senator, it is almost impossible to beat the committee on the floor of the House. This is my third term here and I do not recall any time when the Appropriations Committee has been beaten on any material point.

Senator SMOOT. You want the item for purchase, manufacture, and test of mountain, field, and siege cannon, including their carriages, sites, implements, equipments, and the machinery necessary for their manufacture, from $1,500,000 to $1,750,000?

Mr. DALLINGER. No; to $7,000,000. I want it increased $6,000,000.

Senator SMOOT. Oh, is that all?

Mr. DALLINGER. I do not pretend to be an expert. The officers of the Ordnance Bureau are here, and they know the figures a great deal better than I do, and I do not pretend to know the details. I only know this, as I said before, that you have got to have a very much larger amount than that bill calls for in order to maintain a skeleton organization, and I think it would be a great shame to have that skeleton organization destroyed.

Senator SMOOT. Will the details of this be discussed by you, Gen. Lord?

Gen. LORD. By representatives of the Ordnance Bureau.

Senator SMOOT. Gen. Lord, we will hear from you now.

STATEMENT OF BRIG. GEN. HERBERT M. LORD, DIRECTOR OF FINANCE.

Gen. LORD. Mr. Chairman, I am submitting for the use of the committee a statistical history of this bill in photostat form.

In the first column of figures is the appropriation for 1920.

In the next column is the original estimate printed in the Book of Estimates for 1921.

. In the next column are the revised requirements as finally submitted to the House Committee on Appropriations at the time of the hearing, March 20, 1920.

The next column shows the amounts appropriated in the House bill, and the last column shows the revised requirements, which have the approval of the War Plans Division and the War Department for submission to this committee.

Senator OVERMAN. Let me understand you, General. As I understand, taking the first line of figures, the House appropriated $3,068,100 and you want $3,251,145?

Senator SMOOT. That is for the Engineer Department alone.

Gen. LORD. That is for the Engineer Department alone, under the head of fortifications for continental United States.

Senator OVERMAN. That is the increase you think is absolutely necessary for the Engineer Department?

Gen. LORD. Yes. You will find in studying that table that in many cases they ask for no increase.

Senator SMOOT. The increase asked for the Engineer Department under that item is not $3,251,145, but it is the difference between $3,068,100 and $3,251,145.

Gen. LORD. Yes.

Senator OVERMAN. And that is true as to each item, that the increase asked for represents the difference between the two columns.

Gen. LORD. Yes. In the subsequent sections of this table, A, B, and C, you will find the amounts subdivided and itemized.

On section A will be found the itemized estimates and statistical history for continental United States.

Section B covers the insular possessions and section C the Panama Canal.

The table referred to is as follows:

Statement of estimates for 1921, fortification bill.

(1)	(2)	(3)	(4)	(5)	(6)
General objects.	Appropriation for 1920.	Estimate for 1921.	Revised requirements, Mar. 20, 1920.	Reported by House Appropriations Committee Apr. 9, 1920, and passed by House Apr. 13, 1920.	Revised requirements, Apr. 20, 1920.
Fortifications in the United States (for details see section A):					
Engineer Department	$946,250	$8,328,010	$8,255,858	$3,068,100	$3,251,145
Chief of Coast Artillery		3,136,140	1,699,758	771,685	771,685
Signal Corps	150,000	174,330	174,330	165,000	165,000
Ordnance Department	3,380,442	72,979,880	37,369,636	9,915,933	12,558,733
Construction Division	40,000	559,995	240,027	50,000	50,000
Totals, continental United States	4,516,692	85,178,355	47,739,609	13,970,718	16,796,563
Fortifications in insular possessions (for details see section B):					
Engineer Department	273,750	1,971,000	1,335,760	554,760	1,164,760
Signal Corps	25,000	25,000	25,000	25,000	25,000
Ordnance Department	1,095,000	7,034,865	4,537,960	713,930	713,930
Chief of Coast Artillery		317,350	273,350	175,000	175,000
Construction Division	225,000	374,237	374,237	108,300	108,300
Air Service		2,746,262	2,295,147	1,300,200	1,300,000
Totals, insular possessions	1,618,750	12,468,614	8,841,454	2,877,190	3,486,990

Statement of estimates for 1921, fortification bill—Continued.

(1) General objects.	(2) Appropriation for 1920.	(3) Estimate for 1921.	(4) Revised requirements, Mar. 20, 1920.	(5) Reported by House Appropriations Committee Apr. 9, 1920, and passed by House Apr. 13, 1920.	(6) Revised requirements, Apr. 20, 1920.
Fortification in Panama Canal (for details see section C):					
Engineer Department	$225,000	$910,250	$690,450	$108,750	$664,750
Chief of Coast Artillery		474,001	474,001	474,000	474,000
Signal Corps	10,000	15,000	15,000	15,000	15,000
Ordnance Department	86,000	11,534,494	2,245,777	1,108,684	1,108,684
Construction Division	4,161,849	96,500	96,500	40,000	40,000
Air Service		7,057,516	6,132,823	239,100	2,738,793
Totals, Panama Canal	4,523,849	20,087,761	9,654,551	1,985,534	5,041,227
Board of Ordnance and Fortification		58,500	58,500		
Totals, fortification bill	10,659,291	117,793,330	66,294,114	18,833,442	25,324,780

[Section A.]

CONTINENTAL UNITED STATES.

ENGINEER DEPARTMENT.

General objects.	Appropriation for 1920.	Estimate for 1921.	Revised requirements, Mar. 20, 1920.	Reported by House.	Revised requirements, Apr. 20, 1920.
Gun and mortar batteries	$380,000	$2,900,000	$2,900,000	$1,800,000	$1,800,000
Modernizing older emplacements	37,250	157,510	157,510	37,250	120,295
Preservation and repair of fortifications	250,000	400,000	400,000	300,000	400,000
Plans for fortifications	25,000	25,000	25,000	25,000	25,000
Supplies for seacoast defenses	50,000	75,000	75,000	60,000	60,000
Casemates, galleries, etc., for submarine mines	[1] 400,000	860,000	773,848	150,000	150,000
Sites for fortifications and seacoast defenses		15,000	49,000	49,000	49,000
Land defenses	60,000	20,000		100	100
Electrical and sound-ranging equipment, etc		3,218,500	3,218,500	566,250	566,250
Protecting shore of Sandy Hook Reservation	544,000				
Sea walls and embankments		547,000	547,000	20,500	20,500
Repair and restoration of defenses of Galveston, Tex		10,000	10,000	10,000	10,000
Contingent expenses, seacoast fortifications		100,000	100,000	50,000	50,000
Total	946,250	8,328,010	8,255,858	3,068,100	3,251,145

CHIEF OF COAST ARTILLERY.

General objects.					
Fire control at fortifications		3,134,890	1,698,508	770,000	770,000
Coast Artillery war instruction		1,250	1,250	1,685	1,685
Total		3,136,140	1,699,758	771,685	771,685

SIGNAL CORPS.

General objects.					
Maintenance, etc., fire-control installations at seacoast defenses, Signal Service	150,000	174,330	174,330	165,000	165,000

ORDNANCE DEPARTMENT.

General objects.					
Armament of fortifications:					
B—Mountain, field, and siege cannon (purchase, manufacture, etc.)		15,141,200	11,682,360	1,500,000	2,712,600
C—Mountain, field, and siege cannon (ammunition for)		1,756,000	1,756,000	1,600,000	2,480,200
DFG—Seacoast cannon (purchase, manufacture, etc.)		14,365,400	[2] 5,937,800	2,000,000	2,000,000
H—Seacoast cannon (ammunition for)	855,442	31,596,638	11,505,883	1,000,000	1,000,000
K—Seacoast artillery practice (ammunition, subcaliber guns, etc.)	1,000,000	955,386	217,010	200,000	200,000
M—Seacoast artillery (alteration and maintenance)	1,250,000	3,013,427	1,197,081	1,000,000	1,000,000

[1] Repeal of prior appropriation.　　　[2] Additional contract authorization of $183,600 asked.

Statement of estimates for 1921, fortification bill—Continued.

CONTINENTAL UNITED STATES—Continued.

(1) General objects.	(2) Appropriation for 1920.	(3) Estimate for 1921.	(4) Revised requirements, Mar. 20, 1920.	(5) Reported by House. Appropriations Committee Apr. 9, 1920, and passed by House Apr. 13, 1920.	(6 Revised requirements, Apr. 20, 1920.
ORDNANCE DEPARTMENT—continued.					
Armament of fortifications—Continued.					
L—Mobile artillery (alteration and maintenance)		$3,893,576	$3,607,569	$2,000,000	$2,600,000
N—Mountain, field, and siege artillery practice (ammunition, subcaliber guns, etc.)		105,800	205,800	205,800	205,800
Proving grounds, Army	$400,000	1,563,670	1,200,000	350,000	900,000
Submarine mines:					
A—Procurement of material		528,650			
C—Submarine mine practice (material for)		9,233	9,233	9,233	9,233
B—Maintenance of material	¹125,000	50,900	50,900	50,900	50,900
Total	3,380,442	72,979,880	²37,369,636	9,915,933	12,558,733
CONSTRUCTION DIVISION.					
Barracks and quarters, seacoast defenses	40,000	559,995	240,027	50,000	50,000
AIR SERVICE.					
(Extension of availability of current appropriations asked.)					
Total, continental United States	4,516,692	85,178,355	²47,739,609	13,970,718	16,796,563

[Section B.]

INSULAR POSSESSIONS.

ENGINEER DEPARTMENT.					
Fortifications in insular possessions:					
Preservation and repair of fortifications—					
Hawaiian Islands	$12,500	$15,000	$15,000	$15,000	$15,000
Philippine Islands	35,000	85,800	85,800	50,000	50,000
Searchlights—					
Hawaiian Islands		50,000	50,000	50,000	50,000
Philippine Islands	33,000	2,000	2,000	2,000	2,000
Supplies for seacoast defenses—					
Hawaiian Islands	5,000	7,000	7,000	.7,000	7,000
Philippine Islands	25,000	25,000	25,000	25,000	25,000
Electrical installations—					
Hawaiian Islands	20,000				
Philippine Islands		4,000			
Casements, galleries, etc, for submarine mines—					
Philippine Islands	140,000	102,000	74,000	55,000	55,000
Reserve equipment—					
Hawaiian Islands	3,250				
Philippine Islands		113,200	113,200		
Land defenses—					
Hawaiian Islands		560,000	560,000	130,000	560,000
Philippine Islands		407,000			
Sites for fortifications and seacoast defenses—					
Hawaiian Islands		250,000	205,760	25,760	205,760
Plans for fortifications—					
Hawaiian Islands		3,000	3,000		3,000
Philippine Islands		3,000	3,000	3,000	
Breakwater at Fort Mills, P. I.		152,000			
Engineer wharf, Fort Mills, P. I.		75,000	75,000	75,000	75,000
Seacoast batteries—					
Hawaiian Islands		50,000	50,000	50,000	50,000
Philippine Islands		67,000	67,000	67,000	67,000
Total	273,750	1,971,000	1,335,760	554,760	1,164,760

¹ Repeal of prior appropriation.   ² Additional contract authorization of $183,600 asked.

Statement of estimates for 1921, fortification bill—Continued.

INSULAR POSSESSIONS—Continued.

(1) General objects.	(2) Appropriation for 1920.	(3) Estimate for 1921.	(4) Revised requirements, Mar. 20, 1920.	(5) Reported by House Appropriations Committee Apr. 9, 1920, and passed by House Apr. 13, 1920.	(6) Revised requirements, Apr. 20, 1920.
SIGNAL CORPS.					
Maintenance, etc., fire-control installations at seacoast defenses, insular possessions, Signal Service	$25,000	$25,000	$25,000	$25,000	$25,000
ORDNANCE DEPARTMENT.					
Fortifications in insular possessions:					
DFG—Seacoast cannon (purchase, manufacture, etc.)		2,500,000	718,300	250,000	250,000
H—Seacoast cannon (ammunition for)	1,000,000	3,817,271	3,571,182	250,000	250,000
M—Seacoast Artillery (alteration and maintenance)	125,000	628,664	159,548	125,000	125,000
Submarine mines in insular possessions:					
1—Purchase of material		82,400	82,400	82,400	82,400
2—Maintenance of material	¹ 30,000	6,530	6,530	6,530	6,530
Total	1,095,000	7,034,865	4,537,960	713,930	713,930
CONSTRUCTION DIVISION.					
Seacoast defenses, Philippine Islands and Hawaii	225,000	374,237	374,237	108,300	108,300
CHIEF OF COAST ARTILLERY.					
Fire control in insular possessions		317,350	273,350	175,000	175,000
AIR SERVICE.					
Aviation, seacoast defenses, insular possessions:²					
Purchase, manufacture, etc, of equipment—					
Hawaiian Islands		100	100	100	....
Philippine Islands		100	100	100	....
Establishment, etc., of aviation stations, Hawaiian Islands		2,746,062	2,294,947	1,300,000	1,300,000
Total		2,746,262	2,295,147	1,300,200	1,300,000
Total, insular possessions	1,618,750	12,468,614	8,841,454	2,877,190	3,486,990

[Section C.]

PANAMA CANAL.

ENGINEER DEPARTMENT.					
Maintenance of clearings and trails, Canal Zone, Panama Canal	$30,000	$61,000	$41,200	$30,000	$30,000
Preservation and repair of fortifications, Panama Canal	25,000	31,000	31,000	25,000	25,000
Maintenance of searchlights and electric light and power equipment, Panama Canal	20,000	20,000	20,000	20,000	20,000
Seacoast batteries, Canal Zone, Panama Canal	135,500	20,000	20,000	20,000	20,000
Electric light and power plants, seacoast fortifications. Canal Zone, Panama Canal	20,000	....	....	....	....
Land defenses. Panama Canal	14,000	....	....	....	....
Reserve equipment for fortifications, Panama Canal	7,500	16,000	16,000	7,500	7,500
Searchlights for seacoast fortifications, Canal Zone, Panama Canal		6,000	6,000	....	6,000
Sites for seacoast fortifications, Panama Canal		6,250	6,250	6,250	6,250

¹ Repeal of prior appropriations.   ² Extension of availability of current appropriations also asked.

Statement of estimates for 1921, fortification bill—Continued.

PANAMA CANAL—Continued.

(1) General objects.	(2) Appropriations for 1920.	(3) Estimates for 1921.	(4) Revised requirements Mar. 20, 1920.	(5) Reported by House Appropriation Committee Apr. 9, 1920, and passed by House Apr. 13, 1920.	(6) Revised requirements Apr. 20, 1920.
ENGINEER DEPARTMENT—continued.					
Sea walls and embankments, Panama Canal		$500,000	$500,000		$500,000
Plans for fortifications, Canal Zone, Panama Canal		250,000	50,000		50,000
Total	$252,000	910,250	690,450	$108,750	664,750
CHIEF OF COAST ARTILLERY.					
Fire control, Panama Canal		474,001	474,001	474,000	474,000
SIGNAL CORPS.					
Maintenance, etc., fire-control installations at seacoast defenses, Signal Service, Panama Canal	10,000	15,000	15,000	15,000	15,000
ORDNANCE DEPARTMENT.					
Armanent of fortifications, Panama Canal:					
D. F. G.—Seacoast cannon (purchase, manufacture, etc.)		5,000,000			
H.—Seacoast cannon (ammunition for)		5,751,473	2,137,093	1,000,000	1,000,000
M.—Seacoast Artillery (alteration of)	100,000	407,883	104,546	104,546	104,546
Submarine mines, Panama Canal:					
B.—Alteration, maintenance, etc., of matériel	¹14,000	4,138	4,138	4,138	4,138
A.—Purchase of matériel		371,000			
Total	86,000	11,534,494	2,245,777	1,108,684	1,108,684
CONSTRUCTION DIVISION.					
Army quarters, storehouses, etc., Canal Zone, Panama Canal	4,161,849	96,500	96,500	40,000	40,000
AIR SERVICE.					
Aviation, seacoast defenses, Panama Canal:					
Purchase, manufacture, etc., of equipment		100	100	·100	
Establishment, construction, etc., of aviation stations		7,057,416	6,132,723	239,000	2,738,793
Total		7,057,516	6,132,723	239,100	2,738,793
Total, Panama Canal	4,523,849	20,087,761	9,654,551	1,985,534	5,041,227

¹ Repeal of prior appropriation.

In addition to these increases asked, which will be an increase in the direct appropriations, the Air Service will ask that certain existing appropriations be made available for 1921.

Senator OVERMAN. Does the Air Service come under this bill?

Gen. LORD. They are included in this. They have estimates in this bill.

Senator OVERMAN. This is for fortifications. What are the Air Service appropriations in this bill for?

Gen. LORD. Aviation for seacoast defenses.

Senator SMOOT. Now, General, if you will begin with the bill and take up each item that you want increased, I think we will get along much more rapidly. You can state about them in a general way.

Gen. LORD. I want to call your attention to one item on page 15. It is section 7, at the bottom of the page, a provision that whenever any Government bureau or department procures, by purchase or manufacture, stores or materials of any kind, or performs any service for another bureau or department, the funds of the bureau or department for which the stores or materials are to be procured or the service performed may be placed subject to the requisitions of the bureau or department making the procurement or performing the service for direct expenditure, and that funds so placed shall remain available for expenditure for two years.

The question came up as to whether or not that phraseology would apply to bureaus within one department. There was no question as to its application as between the Interior Department and the War Department, or the Navy Department and the War Department; but the question did arise as to its application as between bureaus of the War Department. That question has been submitted informally to the comptroller's office, and he states that it would apply with equal force to bureaus within the department, as well as to the governmental departments.

Now, with your permission Gen. Rice, who is here representing the Chief of Ordnance, will present the ordnance statement, according to the items, if you desire.

Senator SMOOT. We will hear Gen. Rice.

STATEMENTS OF COL. J. H. RICE, CHIEF OF MANUFACTURE; COL. C. L'H. RUGGLES; COL. G. F. JENKS; AND J. H. PELOT.

Col. RICE. Mr. Chairman, if we may we will discuss first the expenses of ordnance proving grounds, on page 6, line 4 of the bill.

Senator SMOOT. Yes.

Col. RICE. Gen. Ruggles will give you the details of it. We ask for an increase of $550,000.

Senator OVERMAN. On page 6?

Col. RICE. Yes; at the top of the page.

Senator SMOOT. You had $400,000 for the present year?

Col. RICE. Yes.

Col. RUGGLES. With a balance of about $600,000 at the beginning of the year remaining over from the preceding year.

Senator SMOOT. What amount do you want?

Col. RUGGLES. We want $900,000 this year.

Senator SMOOT. Instead of $350,000?

Col. RUGGLES. Instead of $350,000.

Senator SMOOT. Have you any unexpended balance?

Col. RUGGLES. No; we have no unallotted balance except an amount of about $17,000 unallotted. What we mean by that is that when we have our moneys we allot them for various projects to the service. We expect to have no balance on hand at the end of the year. The latest estimates show that it will all be absorbed.

I have here a statement showing the number of rounds we expect to fire at the proving ground next year, why we expect to fire them, and a comparison of the cost at the new proving ground, with that at the old, and an explanation of why we think we need $900,000 instead of $350,000.

During the fiscal year ending June 30, 1921, it is estimated that about 75,000 rounds will be fired at the Aberdeen Proving Ground in the test of matériel completed under Board of Review Projects, in the development of armor-piercing projectiles, the ballistic tests of 12-inch, 14-inch, and 16-inch armor-piercing projectiles, the necessary revision of range tables for seacoast cannon due to essential changes in the rotating band and in the form of the projectile; in the test of experimental guns, carriages, self-propelled mounts, ammunition, fuses, etc., which are being developed in accordance with the recommendation of the Caliber (Westervelt) Board, in the retest of powders, fuses, etc., which may become necessary on account of the irregularities developed in the service at target practice; and in investigating the condition of ammunition now in storage from overseas.

Most of the firing referred to above, whether of matériel furnished under Board of Review Projects, of railway matériel, or of matériel being under the Caliber (Westervelt) Board, will consist in the test of type matériel. If this matériel consisted merely of standard matériel which has been under manufacture for some time and the design of which had been thoroughly tested in the past at the proving ground and in service, the number of rounds to be fired in the test thereof would be limited. Such firing as is done would be in the nature of a precautionary measure as a final check of the inspection which began with the raw material, and would be analogous to the short-road test given the stock automobile at the factory before it is shipped to the purchaser. However, in the test of new types, the Ordnance Department must fire a large number of rounds and go as far in satisfying itself that the new design is right before it can be accepted for service use as the automobile manufacturer goes in the test of a new model of car before he feels safe in placing it on the market.

The test of all new types must be an endurance test to determine whether the functioning of every part of the new mechanism is satisfactory and remains satisfactory throughout the expected life of the gun and carriage. We must assure ourselves that new guns placed in service will not break down by continued use, that the parts of the carriage will not wear so much by continued use that the accuracy of the weapon is affected detrimentally, and that the number of parts requiring replacement due to breakage or wear is not so great as to materially hamper operations in a campaign, etc. The number of rounds to be fired, therefore, is determined primarily by the necessity for giving a proper endurance test to the new design.

Even if no endurance test were necessary, however, each element of the new design must be thoroughly tested, after first adjusting it to assure ourselves that it works efficiently when new and continues so to work during the life of the gun and carriage. Some of the tests required in this connection are as follows:

Determination of the pressure in the recoil mechanism.

Velocity of recoil and counterrecoil.

Time to load and fire a certain number of rounds under different conditions.

Dust and rust test of breech mechanism and carriage.

Accuracy of the gun at various ranges.

Stability of the carriage under all conditions.

Holding ability of spades in various kinds of soil.

Adjustments of variable lengths of recoil.

Satisfactoriness and convenience of manipulation of sights and of elevating and traversing mechanisms.

Convenience of loading and serving the piece at all angles.

Muzzle velocity of projectile.

Pressure in the bore.

Range to be obtained with various charges.

Test of powder, projectiles, and fuzes for the new piece, etc.

In the tests just mentioned, it is not necessary to fire additional rounds, for these tests may be made during the main endurance test of the gun and carriage.

The experience obtained during the war shows not only the desirability of new types of cannon, but the necessity for vastly improving our propelling powders, high explosives, projectiles, and fuzes. Great difficulty was experienced with smokeless powder during the war by reason of its absorption of moisture, causing some shots to fall short and fail to reach the target. The development of a smokeless powder which will not absorb moisture is therefore most desirable and is required by the Caliber (Westervelt) Board. Much difficulty was experienced by all armies from premature bursting of high explosive shell in the bores of the guns, killing the cannoneers serving the piece. The necessity of designing fuzes that will not be subject to this weakness is therefore obvious. About one projectile in 20,000 burst in the bore of the gun during the war, and it is desired to improve the fuze so that this weakness will be entirely eliminated, or at least to reduce the number of premature bursts to a negligible percentage of rounds fired.

The flash which is present when the gun is fired with the smokeless powder used in the war, exposes the position of guns during firing, and it is very necessary to obtain a smokeless powder which will not give this flash. It is a practicable thing to do this, but much experimentation is required. Failure of many high-explosive projectiles to burst on impact, giving what were called " duds," was a very serious feature of the ammunition of all armies. The necessity for perfecting our knowledge of loading high-explosive shell to overcome the large percentage of " duds " is obvious, and this requires many round to be fired at the proving ground. Of course, the vital questions such as have just been mentioned with respect to ammunition, can not be solved by firing a small number of rounds, but here again it is fortunate from the point of view of economy that a large proportion of the rounds necessary for the endurance test of guns and carriages can be utilized in the development of ammunition.

In accordance with the principles explained above, the following table has been prepared showing the contemplated number of rounds to be fired next year at the Aberdeen Proving Ground in the test of new matériel and of old matériel returned from France,

and to investigate irregularities developed in the service at target
practice:

(a) CALIBER BOARD PROJECTS.

Contemplated
number of rounds.

Infantry howitzers, carriages, and ammunition	2, 000
Pack howitzers, carriages and ammunition	2, 000
75-mm. divisional gun on carriage and self-propelled mount and its ammunition	12, 000
105-mm. divisional howitzer on carriage and self-propelled mount and its ammunition	12, 000
4.7-inch corps gun on carriage and self-propelled mount and its ammunition	9, 000
155-mm. corps howitzer on carriage and S. P. mount and its ammunition	9, 000
155-mm. Army gun on carriage and S. P. mount and its ammunition	6, 000
8-inch Army howitzer on carriage and S. P. mount and its ammunition	3, 500
8-inch, 50 caliber gun and railway mount	440
12-inch, 20 caliber howitzer on railway mount	150
14-inch, 50 caliber gun on railway mount	440
16-inch, 25 caliber howitzer and railway mount	200
3-inch antiaircraft gun. self-propelled mount and ammunition	2, 500
4.7-inch antiaircraft gun, self-propelled mount and ammunition	2, 000
Caterpillar adapters for 8-inch howitzer and 155-mm. gun (12 sets for acceptance test)	60
6-inch trench mortars and carriage	1, 000

(b) OTHER THAN CALIBER BOARD PROJECTS.

18 10-inch sliding railway mounts, model 1919	150
12 12-inch railway carriage pivot mounts	110
20 14-inch, 50 caliber guns	80
1 16-inch, 18 caliber howitzer railway carriage pivot mount	30
1 16-inch howitzer barbette carriage, model of 1920 (3)[1]	510
1 16-inch, 50 caliber gun, model of 1919, and 1 16-inch gun barbette carriage, model 1920 (4)[1]	320
1 16-inch, 50 caliber gun, model of 1919, and 1 16-inch disappearing carriage, model of 1917	30
Firings for revision range tables for existing 6, 8, 10, 12, 14 inch guns and 12-inch mortars due to essential changes in rotating band and form of projectile	2, 000
Development of armor-piercing projectiles which will penetrate armor at greater angles of oblique impact than those now in use and of a fuze for these projectiles	375
Ballistic test for acceptance of armor-piercing projectiles:	
12-inch, 54 lots, 4 rounds per lot	216
14-inch, 23 lots, 4 rounds per lot	92
16-inch, 28 lots, 4 rounds per lot	112
Continuation of firings in 3.3-inch gun to determine best shape of projectile, the proper twist of rifling for various shapes, and the general laws of air resistance	5, 000
Proof-firing 37-mm. subcaliber tubes for existing 75-mm., 4.7-inch, and 155-mm. guns, and 155 mm. and 8-inch howitzers	500
For continuance of the development of bombs, bomb sights, fuzes, and release mechanisms, it is contemplated that 3,000 bombs of various types will be dropped.	
Proof-firing 2.24-inch tank gun, test of its mount and ammunition	1, 000
Tests of guns manufactured by the autofrettage process	3, 000
Total	75, 815

The number of rounds the Ordnance Department expects to fire
during the present fiscal year at the Aberdeen Proving Ground is
about 55,000. The reason for the increase in the number of rounds

---

[1] The number in parenthesis indicate the number of units of this type which will be completed during the year.

to 75,000 expected to be fired next year is due to the experimental matériel now being manufactured in accordance with the Caliber (Westervelt) Board project. Practically none of this experimental matériel will be delivered for test this year, and the number of rounds to be fired next year would not be very materially reduced, even if Congress made no further appropriation for experimental work next year.

The great bulk of the work at the Aberdeen Proving Ground is necessarily experimental, and it is very difficult to estimate accurately in advance the cost of each job that may be undertaken, for the reason that the action of the matériel itself, while under test, may vary the cost considerably by prolonging the test or by shortening it. For example, matériel may fail promptly, in which case tests would be suspended; it may not fail entirely, but it may develop unexpected action, which will require further experimenting to discover and remove the cause. In outdoor testing work many delays are caused by unfavorable weather conditions, and so on. For these reasons it has been found necessary, in estimating the cost of proof work at the proving ground, to depend largely on past experience. It can be understood readily that the cost of experimental and development work is much more difficult to estimate than the cost of a determined structure, such as a house, a road, or a machine.

Owing to the fact that during the war and for a considerable part of 1919, enlisted men (drafted men) were used to perform much of the work which is now being done by civilians, it was difficult to form an exact estimate of cost of firing a given number of rounds. Since the drafted army contained many mechanics, engineers, and trained men, enlisted men of this type could do a great deal of work that can not be performed by soldiers in times of peace. Moreover, there are not soldiers available to do this work now, even if they possessed the proper training. The first estimate submitted for the fiscal year 1921 by the commanding officer of the Aberdeen Proving Ground, namely, $2,130,946.51, was so large that it was not accepted by the Ordnance Department and an estimate of $1,563,670.26 was submitted practically against the protest of the commanding officer of the proving ground, who stated it was much too small. Later in the year (in January, 1920), when more information was on hand as to the cost of testing at Aberdeen Proving Ground during the present fiscal year, it was seen that the original estimate submitted was higher than need be and it was therefore reduced to $1,200,000. During March a statement was received from the proving ground as a result of inquiry from this office, showing that the total amount expended for proof purposes up to March 1, 1920, was $925,355.10, with an estimated expenditure for the balance of the fiscal year of $362,089.63, making a total estimated expenditure for the year of $1,287,444.73. The total number of rounds expected to be tested this year is 54,875, which is only a little more than two-thirds of the number of rounds expected to be fired next year. Notwithstanding the estimated expenditure this year of $1,287,444.73 in the test of approximately 55,000 rounds, the estimate for the fiscal year 1921 was further reduced to $900,000 for the test of approximately 75,000 rounds. This was done after consultation with the present commanding officer of the proving ground, who has been there now six and one-half months and who succeeded the commanding officer who objected to the original estimate as being too small. We have been greatly reducing the force at the Aberdeen Proving Ground and increasing the efficiency of the remaining personnel. This is due to discharging the least experienced and least efficient employees, and to the fact that the work can be done more systematically as the confusion resulting from the war and the return to the proving ground of large quantities of matériel used overseas is gradually disappearing.

For many years prior to the late war, the appropriation "Proving Grounds, Army," was only $56,200 annually. For the fiscal year ending June 30, 1917, this was increased to $75,000, and the fortifications act, fiscal year 1918, passed before war was declared, increased this amount to $90,000. These sums were never sufficient to cover the cost of testing at the Sandy Hook Proving Ground, and it was therefore necessary to supplement them by funds from the appropriations for manufacture, which also authorized the test of the matériel manufactured. For next year and thereafter it is proposed to make the appropriation "Proving Grounds, Army," bear all the expenses of test at the Aberdeen Proving Ground; and the estimates submitted under manufacturing appropriations for the fiscal year 1921 do not cover the cost of testing the matériel at the Aberdeen Proving Ground.

Adding to the amounts expended at the Sandy Hook Proving Ground from the appropriation "Proving Ground No. 15" (which was the heading of the appropriation prior to the adoption of the heading "Proving Grounds, Army"), the amounts expended in tests of matériel from manufacturing appropriations, we find that in 1915, $146,525.91 was expended in testing 6,338 rounds, and in 1916, $143,167.92 was expended in testing 6,955 rounds. The cost per round fired was, in 1915, $22.94, and in 1916, $20.58. On the basis of testing 75,000 rounds next year, at a cost of $900,000, the cost per round fired would be $12, and this notwithstanding the fact that $1 now is worth not over 50 cents as compared with 1916. The cost per round includes overhead charges, and these charges do not increase in proportion to the increase of the number of rounds fired. A comparison, however, should show that we are contemplating doing our work very economically as compared with what we did before the war.

Allowing for the decrease in the value of the dollar, about $300,000 during the fiscal year 1921 will be equivalent to approximately $143,000 expended in testing 6,955 rounds at the Sandy Hook Proving Ground in 1916. In asking for $900,000 to cover the cost of testing at the Aberdeen Proving Ground during the fiscal year 1921, the Ordnance Department therefore is asking only for about three times the present equivalent of the amount expended in 1916 at the Sandy Hook Proving Ground and expects to fire with the sum asked over ten times as many rounds as it did at the Sandy Hook Proving Ground in 1916. The 1921 fortifications bill, as passed by the House of Representatives includes an item of $350,000 under "Proving grounds, Army," instead of $900,000 as last estimated by the Ordnance Department. This amount is altogether inadequate for the work on the Aberdeen Proving Ground next year if the matériel now under development is to be tested and if we are to profit by experience gained during the war; it is but little more than twice the sum expended at the Sandly Hook Proving Ground before the war, and it is now thoroughly appreciated that the number of rounds fired at the Sandy Hook Proving Ground before the war was not sufficient to keep our progress in ordnance up to date.

In comparing the cost of operation on a very much reduced scale at the Aberdeen Proving Ground, such as would be required if only $350,000 be available for the work there, with the cost of operation of the Sandy Hook Proving Ground, which has now been abandoned, it must be taken into consideration that the Sandy Hook Proving Ground was altogether inadequate for the work and that a much larger proving ground has been acquired to take its place. The area covered is much greater necessitating a much larger amount of railroad trackage. very much longer heating, lighting, and power mains, a much larger water supply, larger shops, and a larger power plant. To minimize the results of a possible accident and to prevent one test interfering with another, the various firing batteries at the Aberdeen Proving Ground have been widely separated, which was not possible at the Sandy Hook Proving Ground. When operating on a large scale, the overhead cost of these facilities at the Aberdeen Proving Ground is smaller than the overhead cost of similar facilities at the Sandy Hook Proving Ground when operating on a small scale, but when operating on a small scale at the Aberdeen Proving Ground the cost of keeping the larger facilities in shape for even a minimum operation will be much greater than was the case at Sandy Hook. It can not be considered, therefore, taking into account the decreased value of the dollar and the larger plant at Aberdeen that $350,000 for the fiscal year 1921 is equivalent to $143,167.22 spent at the Sandy Hook Proving Ground in 1916.

In view of the arguments set forth above, it is requested that the Committee on Appropriations of the Senate increase the item of $350,000 for "Proving grounds, Army," allowed by the House of Representatives to the $900,000 last estimated by the Ordnance Department.

Estimate for fiscal year 1921, proving grounds, Army.

	Original estimate.	Revised estimate.
Services of assistants to the Ordnance board....................................	$2,850.00	....
Services of employees engaged in current work including skilled mechanical labor..	68,958.00	$38,974.80
Services, materials, and supplies required for the maintenance of proving ground patrol boats and steamers..	18,280.00	10,968.00
Services, materials, and supplies required for the maintenance of railroad transportation...	248,417.26	146,050.20
Services, material, and supplies required for making repairs and alterations incidental to testing and proving ordnance and ordnance stores, including repairing butts and targets and grading ranges already established........	147,165.20	86,799.12
Purchase of instruments and other supplies..	15,000.00	9,000.00
Test of mobile and seacoast artillery matériel and ammunition, including maintenance of heating and refrigerating plant..............................	979,815.00	585,297.00
Tests of hand grenades, bombs, bomb-dropping devices and aerial devices..	83,184.80	22,910.85
Total...	1,563,670.26	900,000.00

In brief, Mr. Chairman, we estimate that we have now work under development which will require us to fire 75,000 rounds at the proving ground next year, and we are asking for $900,000, which is about $12 per round.

The cost of experimental work is difficult to estimate. The number of rounds is difficult to estimate, and the cost is difficult to estimate, because, being experimental, the circumstances of each test may vary. Something unexpected may happen which will prolong a test. So we base our estimate on experience.

At the Sandy Hook Proving Ground it cost us $22 to $24 per round, and we only fired about 7,000 rounds per year, which from our present experience was altogether too small. We did not progress in ordnance before the war as we should have had we been more liberal in our experimental work at the proving grounds.

As a result of this uncertainty, the first estimate submitted from the proving ground this year was for over $2,000,000. In the Ordnance Office we felt that that was a great deal too high, and we reduced it to $1,563,670.26.

Then, later on in the year, when we found how our expenses were running, we were able to cut that down to $1,200,000. Then, in March we took another view of the situation, found out what the work was costing then, and determined that we could reduce that amount to $900,000.

Senator SMOOT. Let me ask you a question, Colonel; is this $900,000 based upon an estimate of $24 per round?

Col. RUGGLES. It is based on an estimate of $12 per round, which is approximately half what it cost us at Sandy Hook. The reason for that is the larger number of rounds to be fired, and the fact that this appropriation bears not only the cost of the actual firing at the guns, but the overhead, the running expenses of the proving ground, the railroad, the power, and the light and heat.

From our records we find that in the last two years before the war we spent approximately $150,000 a year at Sandy Hook. That is equivalent now to something over $300,000, and we did an amount of testing that was admittedly too small, and we had not the problems before us then that we have now. We did not know as much about ordnance then as we do now, and we have learned of a great many lines along which a further advance is absolutely imperative if we are to keep up with what other nations will do because of the experience of the war. The experience of the war shows how our material can be improved. That $150,000 in 1915–16 is about equivalent to $300,000 now.

The Aberdeen Proving Ground is a very much larger establishment than Sandy Hook. It had to be, because Sandy Hook was very much too small. Sandy Hook Proving Ground was established in 1874 as a temporary expedient, but we were never able to get away from it until the war broke out, when the necessity for a larger proving ground was seen. As a result of the larger proving ground and larger plant it will cost us more to operate that big plant than it would the small one, and my estimate is that about $450,000 at the Aberdeen Proving Ground in 1921 will do only the amount of work that $150,000 did at Sandy Hook in 1916, because of the difference in the value of the dollar and the difference in the size of the establishments.

Senator OVERMAN. Where is the Aberdeen Proving Ground?

Col. RUGGLES. It is at Aberdeen, Md. We are asking for $900,000, which is approximately twice what I think it would cost us to operate at Aberdeen proving ground on the same basis as we operated at the Sandy Hook proving ground before the war. We are expecting, however, to do ten times as much work. If we do not have $900,000, it will be impossible for us to test the material that is now under development. The material that is now being manufactured, costing hundreds of thousands and even millions of dollars, will have to wait, perhaps for a year, before it can be tested. Some of it can be tested with $350,000, but a relatively small amount.

Senator OVERMAN. Is that where you test out the materials furnished to the Army, to see whether they come up to the standard?

Col. RUGGLES. At the proving ground we test all of our cannon of all calibers and all ammunition for cannon. It is the place where we do all testing of that kind for the Ordnance Department.

The number of improvements that are projected is very great. We learned lots of things during the war that we never expected. There is the matter of projectiles for one thing. We had been accustomed to firing at an angle of 15° elevation or less, and at those angles of elevation the projectile acted pretty well. The pattern was sufficiently concentrated. That is, the shots did not spread too much as they struck, and the range we thought was pretty good. That was because the peculiar effect of the air on projectiles is not so marked by any means under the angle of 15° elevation as it is when we get up to an angle of 45° or even over 20°. We found out that the points of our projectiles were wrong, that the shapes of our projectiles were wrong; not worse than those of our allies, but all projectiles were wrongly made. It is astonishing what differences in the flight of projectiles little changes in the shape of the point and the base and the shape of the band will make.

We can increase our ranges 20 or even 40 per cent, and we can reduce the spread of our shots at the target by from 50 to 90 per cent by changes in the shape of projectiles. That is one of the things that we are now investigating, which we expect to do next year.

These experiments, as I say, will increase the value of our armament very much, because of the longer range and better accuracy to be obtained thereby.

Unfortunately, what you find out for one caliber of projectile does not apply to all, so that these experiments have to be continued with respect to all calibers.

The matter of fuses is another thing. We were forced to use the French fuse during the war for reasons of policy, and our development of fuses p a   a   stopped. We know that the French fuses were unsafe. A great many guns were blown up during the war, and we know how to develop a fuse that will not do that, but it requires a large amount of experimental work which is now going on, and we have to fire a large number of those fuses at our proving ground, to try out variations of one kind and another until we get them perfected.

The seacoast fuse is in the same condition. We find that our seacoast fuses are breaking up on impact against armor. We do not have as long a delay as we ought to have before the fuze acts after the projectile strikes the armor. The Battle of Jutland showed that.

A long delay is required to enable the projectile to pierce the armor and reach the vitals of the ship before exploding. A large series of experiments will have to be carried on on our seacoast fuses.

All these improvements must be applied to the armament that we now have with troops and in store.

In addition to this we know how we can improve our guns very materially, and the War Department has ordered that this development be made; and we have under manufacture a large number of new cannon and new carriages, which we can not test if we do not have more than $350,000 for the proving ground next year. So that we will have done a large part of the work, but we can not finish it.

Senator SMOOT. Colonel, you do not believe we are going to have eternal peace from now on in the world?

Col. RUGGLES. No, sir; I do not.

Senator SMOOT. Sensible man! Is there anything else?

Col. RUGGLES. Nothing except to say this, Mr. Chairman, that before the war this appropriation was very small, and we suplemented it by using appropriations for the manufacture of materials. Now, we want to get away from that. We think that the expenses at the proving ground should be borne by an appropriation for that purpose.

So when I speak of $150,000 being spent annually at the proving ground before the war, it was made up of about $56,000 from this appropriation plus approximately $100,000 from the appropriations for the manufacture of the articles that were tested. We do not want to do that in the future. We want to confine the cost of tests at the proving ground to this appropriation, and in the estimates that have been submitted for the experimental material the cost of testing at the proving ground has been omitted, so that there will be no question of duplicating that cost. This appropriation was gradually increased up to $90,000 before the war, but that was small compared with the total cost of testing.

Col. RICE. Mr. Chairman, I would like to have Col. Jenks explain the details of the amount that we wish to ask for in the item beginning with line 18, on page 4, armament of fortifications. We are asking for an increase of $1,221,600.

STATEMENT OF COL. G. F. JENKS, CHIEF OF THE ARTILLERY DIVISION.

Col. RICE. Col. Jenks is Chief of the Artillery Division, and has charge of artillery in the office of the Chief of Ordnance.

Senator SMOOT. Col. Jenks wishes to refer to the item beginning with line 18, on page 4, armament of fortifications.

Col. RICE. Yes, sir.

Senator SMOOT. The same item that was spoken of by Representative Dallinger?

Col. RICE. One item that Mr. Dallinger mentioned, yes.

Senator SMOOT. What is the increase of appropriation?

Col. RICE. From $1,500,000 to $2,712,600, an increase of $1,212,600.

Col. JENKS. Mr. Chairman, the estimate submitted to the House under this appropriation was $11,682,360.

That estimate was based on carrying on certain production work, certain experimental work, and of initiating certain new production of material.

The amount of funds asked for for carrying on experimental and production work was based on the use of certain funds from current appropriations, which was explained on page 208 of the hearings before the House committee as being approximately $1,200,000, that sum being what was estimated would be allotted before June 30 for work under new orders, and did not include what might be required as additional amounts to complete old orders and for which we had assumed sufficient funds had been allotted but for which we may find it necessary to allot additional funds.

Senator SMOOT. Colonel, if there is anything new that you think of that you did not testify before the House committee, I wish you would emphasize those items. We have your testimony before the House committee on page 208, and I take it for granted that your testimony is the same covering the points as to which you there testified.

Col. JENKS. Yes, sir.

Senator SMOOT. If there is anything further that you have to say by way of additional reasons or evidence, I wish you would confine yourself to that as nearly as possible.

Col. JENKS. Yes, sir. I wish to explain briefly that in closing out some of the war orders we will find that in some cases we have surplus funds, in which case they will go back to the Treasury. In other cases we will find that our estimates of the amount of money that we placed for certain manufactures will be too small, that we will require small amounts in addition. It was impossible to foresee those when the estimate was made to the House, and we will require small amounts of funds to be allotted in addition to the $1,200,000 testified to before the House committee, which were not considered in that testimony.

Senator SMOOT. What would they amount to, in your opinion?

Col. JENKS. I have no statement of that, Mr. Chairman, because it is impossible to tell now what the arsenals are going to require.

Senator SMOOT. You have some idea, haven't you?

Col. JENKS. It will be comparatively small.

Now, the estimates which we are resubmitting under this appropriation are based on the use of $1,000,000 additional funds under war appropriations, under armament of fortifications, " B." This amount has not yet been allotted, but the chairman of the subcommittee of the House Appropriations Committee suggested that if we obtained the approval of the use of $1,000,000 more of current funds under the appropriation armament of fortifications, B, no criticism of such use would be made by that subcommittee.

Section 6 of the House bill permits orders to be placed with arsenals and allows funds to be used after June 30. The estimates which we now submit are based on the use of this $1,000,000 additional amount under this appropriation.

The House estimates included $3,000,000 for the new production of artillery material, which was an item for 12 railway mounts. We have been informed by the chairman of the subcommittee that the subcommittee intended to appropriate sufficient funds to complete one pilot 14-inch railway mount and to inaugurate work on two additional mounts, and we now submit an estimate on that basis.

The construction of the pilot mount is included in the item which I will take up later for development work, and we expect to do only $80,000 worth of work on the procurement of material for two mounts, after the construction and test of the pilot.

For the development of artillery material, including design and manufacture of pilots, experimental work, and the manufacture of material for service tests, the estimates submitted to the House call for $5,805,760.

The estimates now being submitted call for $2,343,600. Of that amount, $1,548,600 is for the experimental work on artillery material and aircraft cannon. The sum of $795,000 is for experimental work on tractor material and the manufacture of certain tractor material for service tests. Col. Moody can explain the details of that much better than I can.

For the continuation of production of artillery material the amount asked for before the House was $725,000. This item is reduced to $289,000, which conforms with the policy outlined by the chairman of the subcommittee. That item covers certain works connected with the storage and preservation of jigs and fixtures which have been made by manufacturers of war material during the war, and which are being stored or preserved at Government arsenals.

It also includes the continuation of work on some 14-inch guns which were ordered during the war as a war order and which were continued in manufacture.

The revised estimates on the 14-inch guns are based on the completing of those guns in three or four years instead of completing the order in the second year in accordance with the estimates submitted by the House.

The total amount covered by this estimate is $2,712,600.

The large item on this work is that for the experimental work on artillery material, $1,548,600.

The program which we submitted to the House is contained on page 227 of the House hearings.

Senator SMOOT. Colonel, will you take a copy of the bill and turn to page 4, because the figures that you have quoted do not correspond in any way with the estimates that we have here in the committee, and, really, I could not follow you there, so I think you had better let me ask you some questions, so that we will get at this thing, so I will understand it. The other members of the committee may have understood it.

Senator HARRIS. I did not.

Senator SMOOT. The House gave you $1,500,000 for the purchase, manufacture, and test of mountain, field, and siege cannon, and so forth.

Col. JENKS. Yes, sir.

Senator SMOOT. As I understand you, you want $2,700,000?

Col. JENKS. We want $2,712,600.

Senator SMOOT. What was the estimate?

Col. JENKS. Do you mean the estimate submitted to the House, or the revised estimate?

Senator SMOOT. I would rather have the revised estimate.

Col. JENKS. The revised estimate on that is $80,000, to inaugurate the work on two railway mounts, in addition to a pilot mount; $2,343,600 for experimental work for the development of artillery and tractor matériel, and $289,000 for continuation of production on artillery matériel and the preservation of jigs and fixtures.

Senator SMOOT. The next item, on page 4, line 22, is for purchase, manufacture, maintenance, and test of ammunition for mountain, field, and siege cannon, including the necessary experiments in connection therewith, the necessary machinery for its manufacture, and necessary storage facilities. The House gave you $1,600,000. What do you ask?

Col. RICE. Mr. Chairman, I thought we were asked for the revised estimate as submitted to the House of Representatives.

Senator SMOOT. I want the revised estimates.

Col. RICE. The revised estimate as given to the House in the original appropriation was something over $11,000,000.

Senator OVERMAN. The evidence that you have given refers to page 4, between lines 18 and 21, $1,500,000?

Col. JENKS. Yes, sir.

Senator OVERMAN. That is included in everything you have said?

Col. JENKS. Yes, sir. .

Senator OVERMAN. Except that you want it increased from $1,500,-000 to $2,712,600.

Col. JENKS. Yes, sir.

Senator OVERMAN. That covers what you have said.

Col. JENKS. Yes, sir.

Senator SMOOT. I notice here on this statement submitted by Gen. Lord that the amount of the revised estimate is $2,712,600 as reported by you. Now the next item, for mountain, siege, and field cannon, under that paragraph the House gave you $1,600,000, and your revised estimate is $2,480,200.

Col. RICE. Yes, sir; that is another heading.

Senator SMOOT. It is the same item as mentioned in this bill?

Col. RICE. Yes, sir; it is the same item, but that is not the same item that Col. Jenks was defending.

Senator SMOOT. I want to get that so we will know where we are at. Instead of $1,600,000 for the purchase, manufacture, maintenance, and testing of ammunition, etc., you want $2,480,200?

Col. RICE. Yes, sir.

Senator SMOOT. The next item, beginning at line 3, on page 5, is for the purchase, manufacture, and test of seacoast cannon for coast defense.

Col. RICE. We are not asking for any increase on these other items, except these two and the one that Gen. Ruggles has defended.

Senator SMOOT. Then Representative Dallinger asked that we increase that to $2,910,000.

Col. RICE. Yes, sir.

Senator SMOOT. What have you to say about that? In your revised estimates $2,000,000 is all you have asked.

Col. RICE. That was in accordance with the War Department policy as established at the meeting of the War Plans Division. It would be very much better from every standpoint if we could get the full appropriation.

Senator Overman. But you could get along with $2,000,000?

Col. Rice. Not at all satisfactorily.

Senator Smoot. From your revised estimate, the increases which you desire are on the first item, for purchase, manufacture, and test of mountain, field, and siege cannon, from $1,500,000 to $2,712,600; and for purchase, manufacture, maintenance, and test of ammunition for mountain, field, and siege cannon, you want an increase from $1,600,000 to $2,480,200?

Col. Rice. Yes, sir.

Senator Smoot. And that covers the increases you desire to ask for, for armament of fortifications?

Col. Rice. Except the one for proving grounds, which has been presented.

Senator Smoot. That was by Gen. Ruggles?

Col. Rice. Yes, sir.

Senator Smoot. All right. I think we understand the situation. Who else have you got?

Col. Rice. Is that all you wish on this item?

Senator Smoot. I think that is all, unless you have something else you wish to present.

Col. Rice. I think there is one other thing we would like to mention.

Col. Jenks. In the testimony before the House committee, given on page 227 of the House hearings, we submitted a program for experimental work. These estimates are based on a very much reduced program—the completion of the manufacture of pilot material which is now under manufacture and the inauguration of manufacture of a few pilots of artillery material which are now under study.

Senator Overman. Please explain to me what you mean by pilot material.

Col. Jenks. The artillery material we have on hand now, which was manufactured during the war, is of designs which were current before the war. The service is not at all satisfied with these designs, and they have called on us to develop artillery material which will give very much greater ranges than that now obtained.

In order to develop this material, it is first necessary for us to study it on the drawing board and prepare a design.

The next stage in the development is to construct a wooden model in accordance with that design, and after the wooden model has been corrected and the drawings corrected, then we manufacture the pilot material. That is a sample piece which is especially for testing at the proving ground to determine whether that material meets certain engineering conditions—that is, whether it meets the conditions that have been laid down by the service, and whether the material and the construction employed are satisfactory mechanically. After the construction of the pilot material we will undoubtedly find many faults and experience many troubles, and it will be necessary for us to redesign the matériel and construct a new pilot. After we have obtained a satisfactory pilot, then the next stage in the development is to submit that material to a service test.

In our original program submitted to the House we had expected to go forward and complete the test of some of this pilot matériel and redesign it, and even to start on the manufacture of some matériel for service tests; but in view of the ideas of the House committee we very much reduced this program, and the estimates now submitted are on the basis of carrying this program out over a greater number of years; but it will be necessary to accomplish the same results in order to satisfy the service and give them the type of matériel which they require.

Senator OVERMAN. Your original estimate was $11,000,000, was it?

Col. JENKS. The estimate for this particular item was $5,800,000.

Senator OVERMAN. And you reduced it at the suggestion of the House to the amount you now ask?

Col. JENKS. Yes, and this is based on a reduced program of not attempting to develop certain classes of matériel this year, but merely the completing of those which we have now started, and which we have so far advanced that they will be ready for the construction of the pilots. The details of these items are shown in the following table:

Tentative apportionment of funds for experimental work covered in estimates for fiscal year 1921 given in hearing before Senate Appropriation Committee, based on the use of current funds as stated during hearings.

FOR ARTILERY MATÉRIEL.

	Amount.
75-mm. field gun matériel	$10,000
105-mm. field howitzer matériel	10,000
75-mm. mountain howitzer matériel	16,900
4.7-inch field gun matériel	9,000
155-mm. howitzer matériel	21,500
4.7-inch gun caterpillar matériel	51,000
155-mm. howitzer caterpillar matériel	51,000
155-mm. gun matériel	7,000
8-inch howitzer matériel	84,000
240-mm. howitzer matériel	105,000
4.7-inch antiaircraft caterpillar matériel	163,000
4.7-inch anticraft matériel, Christie type	78,000
Infantry howitzer matériel	56,000
Miscellaneous work	51,200
8-inch railway gun and mount	41,000
14-inch railway mount	220,000
16-inch howitzer and parts of railway mount	40,000
Drafting and engineering work	250,000
Auto frettage guns and experimental work	80,000
6-inch trench mortars	9,000
Sights and fire-control matériel	40,000
Wire wrapped experimental guns	60,000
Aircraft armament matériel	25,000
Total	1,548,600

FOR TRACTOR MATÉRIEL.

Light armor plate	20,000
Service test 1½-ton caterpillar trailer	36,000
Service test 3-ton caterpillar trailer	39,000
Tractor for divisional artillery	40,000
Tractor caisson for divisional artillery	20,000
Tractor for corps artillery	20,000
Tractor caisson for corps artillery	20,000
Tractor for Army artillery	25,000
Tractor caisson for Army artillery	25,000
Trailer caisson for Army artillery	10,000

Amount.

Service test of motor equipment for 75-mm. gun in batteries (partial equipment for four batteries)	$250, 000
Tractor for specially heavy artillery	30, 000
Tractor caisson, ½ ton	20, 000
Tractor power cart	20, 000
Caterpillar hand cart	5, 000
Service test hand caterpillar cart	5, 000
Engineering and drafting	150, 000
Service test, ½-ton tractor	36, 000
Service test, tractor power cart	24, 000
Total	795, 000
Grand total for experimental and development work	2, 343, 600

In the above all estimates included in the estimates submitted to the House for pilots "not initiated on June 30, 1920" (see p. 227 of hearing before the subcommittee of House Committee on Appropriations, 1920), have been omitted except in the case of the Infantry howitzer and trench mortar. Those items in which a saving in development cost might be expected by delay in initiating work have been omitted. Estimates on other projects are based on a smaller amount of work being done on the project.

The estimate does not include any funds allotted or to be allotted during the current fiscal year or those which may be required to complete work after the fiscal year 1921.

The number of types of pilot or sample vehicles has been reduced to a minimum, usually only one being included in the estimate.

In previous estimate the item for drafting work was included in the amount estimated under each project.

Senator SMOOT. Whom else do you desire to call?

Col. RICE. Col. Pelot, chief of the ammunition division of the office of the chief of manufacture.

Senator OVERMAN. Referring to what page of the bill?

Col. RICE. The next item on page 4.

Senator SMOOT. For the purchase, maintenance, and manufacture of materials for mountain, field, and siege cannon?

Col. RICE. Yes, sir; ammunition.

STATEMENT OF COL. J. H. PELOT.

Senator SMOOT. Col. Pelot, the full committee meets at 11 o'clock, and we have only a few minutes more, and we would like to have you cover as many items as possible in that short time.

Col. PELOT. The Ordnance Department originally submitted to Congress an estimate of $1,756,000—

For purchase, manufacture, and test of ammunition for mountain, field, and siege cannon, including the necessary experiments in connection therewith and the machinery necessary for its manufacture, and necessary storage facilities.

This estimate did not include any funds for maintenance of the large quantities of artillery ammunition on hand; therefore an estimate of $1,244,200 was presented in the hearings on the Army bill before the House Committee on Military Affairs to cover maintenance.

The Military Affairs Committee considered that this item in the estimates belonged in the fortifications bill, and it was therefore necessary to request the House Committee on Appropriations to give us $1,244,200 in addition to the original estimate of $1,756,000.

Senator SMOOT. Maintenance for what?

Col. PELOT. One million two hundred and forty-four thousand two hundred dollars for maintenance of ammunition constituting the reserve.

That leaves us then but $355,800 to carry on experimental and development work on ammunition for mobile artillery. We are now asking you for a total appropriation of $2,480,200, which is an increase of $880,200 over the amount appropriated by the House, but $520,000 less than the total estimate presented to the House.

The additional amount we are requesting is to be used for experimental and development work in order that we may avail ourselves now of the experience and knowledge that we have gained during the war before the information slips away from us and before all our experienced personnel have left us. The items on which the funds would be used for experimental work are as follows:

Ammunition Division.—Estimate of funds required under A. of F. "C" for experimental work for the fiscal year July 1, 1920, to June 30, 1921—Summary.

For the development of a mechanical time fuse	$100,000
For the development of a point-detonating fuse and base fuse for mobile artillery ammunition	150,000
For the development of primers	10,000
For the development of cartridge cases	20,000
For the development of common steel shell	150,000
For the development of semisteel shell	60,000
For the development of chemical shell	150,000
For the development of propellant powders	185,000
For the development of high explosives	80,000
For raw materials and chemicals	40,000
For experimental loadings and firings for field, railway, antiaircraft, and trench mortar ammunition	230,000
For the experimental manufacture and test of projectiles to determine the form of maximum ballistic efficiency	50,000
For the purchase and manufacture of experimental steel for test	11,000
Total	1,236,000

Senator SMOOT. I think that will cover the case, when we take into consideration your testimony before the House committee. If there is anything special that you desire to call attention to other than what was in your testimony before the House committee, you may state that. I think we have your desires in mind and know just about what you want. Is there anything else you desire to go into?

Col. PELOT. I would like to make a statement, sir, of the contemplated obligations from the present funds before June 30 of this year, which is a total of $1,671,366.

Senator SMOOT. That is for obligations that you have entered into between now and June 30 of this year?

Col. PELOT. Yes; obligations we expect to enter into; that is only for the manufacturing divisions. It does not include any obligations that will be entered into due to salvaging of war material and preservation of war materials or settlements of claims, transportation, and a number of other items of that kind. It simply covers the obligations for experimental work, for the providing of facilities for experimental work at Picatinny arsenal, and providing the expenses for personnel and other operating expenses, etc., at five of our arsenals for the last quarter of this fiscal year.

UNEXPENDED BALANCES.

Col. RICE. As to the amount of money to be turned in, we would like to have plenty of time on that. That is on page 16 of the bill.

Senator SMOOT. Is that the last item you want to discuss?

Col. RICE. No, sir; we have two items of special legislation in addition that we wish to present.

Senator SMOOT. Then perhaps we had better suspend at this time.

Whereupon, at 11 a. m., the committee went into executive session.

(At 12 o'clock the committee adjourned until Friday, April 23, 1920, at 10 o'clock a. m.)

FORTIFICATIONS APPROPRIATION BILL, 1921.

SUBCOMMITTEE OF THE COMMITTEE ON APPROPRIATIONS,
UNITED STATES SENATE,
Washington, D. C.

The subcommittee met at 10 o'clock a. m.

Present: Senators Smoot (chairman) and Overman.

FURTHER STATEMENT OF COL. J. H. RICE, UNITED STATES ARMY, CHIEF OF MANUFACTURE, ORDNANCE DEPARTMENT.

Senator SMOOT. Col. Rice, you may proceed.

ORDERS PLACED WITH GOVERNMENT ESTABLISHMENTS.

Col. RICE. I wish to speak first in regard to section 6, on page 15 of the committee print. That provision is intended to accomplish certain things, and since it was submitted to the fortifications subcommittee of the House Appropriations Committee we find by informal consultation with the comptroller that it really will not accomplish what was intended. I therefore ask for a change in the wording, to read as follows:

> That all orders or contracts for the manufacture of material pertaining to approved projects heretofore or hereafter placed with Government-owned establishments shall be considered as obligations in the same manner as provided for similar orders placed with commercial manufacturers, and the appropriations shall remain available for the payment of the obligations so created, as in the case of contracts or orders with commercial manufacturers.

The hearings before the House committee give a fairly full explanation, so I will not go into it further than to say that it is for the purpose of putting into effect in proper language the intention of that provision.

Senator SMOOT. Proceed.

EMPLOYMENT OF SERVICE IN DISTRICT OF COLUMBIA.

Col. RICE. There was a provision carried in the original proposed bill as submitted to the fortifications subcommittee which was not carried in the bill as reported to the House. It is very important to the Ordnance Department, and we wish to recommend that it be reinstated, if possible. It reads as follows:

> The Chief of Ordnance of the United States Army is authorized to employ in the District of Columbia, out of the appropriations made in this act for designing, procuring, caring for, and supplying ordnance and ordnance stores to the Army,

such services, other than clerical, as are necessary for carrying out these purposes, and the act making appropriations for the legislative, executive, and judicial expenses of the Government for the fiscal year ending June 30, 1921, is amended accordingly; *Provided*, That the entire expenditures for this purpose for the fiscal year 1921 shall not exceed $142,900.

Senator SMOOT. I notice there is an explanation here of the suggested amendment. That covers the object of the proposed provision?

Col. RICE. Yes, sir. I have here a brief statement which, if you do not mind, I should like to give to the stenographer to put in the record.

Senator SMOOT. Yes; put it in the record.

(The statement is as follows:)

WAR DEPARTMENT,
OFFICE OF THE CHIEF OF ORDNANCE,
Washington, April 21, 1920.

Mr. CHAIRMAN: It is desired to incorporate the following amendment in this bill:

"The Chief of Ordnance of the United States Army is authorized to employ in the District of Columbia, out of the appropriations made in this act for designing, procuring, caring for, and supplying ordnance and ordnance stores to the Amy, such services, other than clerical, as are necessary for carrying out these purposes, and the act making appropriations for the legislative, executive, and judicial expenses of the Government for the fiscal year ending June 30, 1921, is amended accordingly: *Provided*, That the entire expenditures for this purpose for the fiscal year 1921 shall not exceed $142,000."

This legislation was first carried in the urgent deficiency appropriation act approved June 15, 1917, and has since been repeated in the urgent deficiency act approved October 6, 1917, and the Army appropriations acts approved July 9, 1918, and July 11, 1919. It has been introduced in the estimates for this bill for the first time this year, for the reason that it was thought to be legislation more properly applicable to this bill than to the Army bill, since this bill is acted upon by the same committees in Congress as act on the legislative, executive, and judicial bill, in which appropriations are made for the remainder of our civilian personnel employed in Washington.

It is desired to emphasize the fact that this provision does not require the appropriation of any additional funds. It is considered necessary for two principal reasons. First, it is impossible to employ certain experts which the Ordnance Department requires for salaries not exceeding $1,800, which is the limit placed on our additional and statutory rolls. The mechanical engineers, ordnance engineers, ballisticians, mathematical experts, etc., who are all carried on the District of Columbia nonclerical roll, must be employed in addition to the regular officers of the Ordnance Department if the department is going to exist as a competent, vigorous, and up-to-date branch of the War Department. Secondly, in the legislative, executive, and judicial bill, as passed, a prohibition is made against the payment of civilian personnel in bureaus or offices of the War Department in the District of Columbia from funds provided in any other act for the fiscal year 1921, with two exceptions which do not affect the Ordnance Department. That is why the wording of the last part of the requested amendment is desired.

It is true that the so-called allotment roll provides for the employment of skilled draftsmen and such other services as the Secretary of War may deem necessary in the opinion of the Chief of Ordnance. This roll has, however, for several years been practically limited to draftsmen, and the Ordnance Department estimate for this year was on this basis. This estimate totaled $660,000. but only $400,000 was appropriated, so it is obvious that the Ordnance Department can not keep the drafting force deemed necessary by it, and much less can it add to this roll civilian experts of the class previously mentioned.

Four hundred thousand dollars was appropriated for this year and it is expected to spend it all. Besides, in order to keep up current drafting work, it has been necessary to transfer considerable of this work to arsenals, at loss of speed and economy. because there were not sufficient funds to hire the necessary number of draftsmen in the District of Columbia.

On March 15, 1920, there were carried on the District of Columbia nonclerical roll: 1 employee, at $5,000; 5 employees, at from $4,000 to $4,500; 9 employees, at from $3,000 to $3,500; 11 employees, at from $2,500 to $2,900; 49 employees, at from $2,000 to $2,400; 42 employees, at less than $2.000; total, 117; 3 special per diem, under personal-service contracts, 120.

It is estimated that for this year the total amount to be expended on this roll will be approximately $260,000. We estimate that for next year, for the class of employees engaged on nonclerical work and of a type which can not be obtained for $1,800 per year, we will require about $142,900.

It is conscientiously believed that, for the Ordnance Department to properly fulfill its functions, this amendment is necessary and its adoption is most earnestly requested.

Col. RICE. There is a change in it, putting the limitation on the amount. I should like to say that it covers the employment of experts in the Ordnance Department, and we consider it absolutely essential that we get it if we are going to function properly.

I am going to ask Col. Gatchell now to give you information in regard to the recovery feature carried on page 16, the first item being in line 20.

STATEMENT OF COL. O. J. GATCHELL, UNITED STATES ARMY.

SURPLUS FUNDS, WAR CONTRACTS.

Col. GATCHELL. Mr. Chairman, in the hearings before the Appropriations Committee of the House of Representatives, with reference to the fortifications bill, a statement was submitted showing the surplus funds which the Ordnance Department expected to have from war appropriations under fortifications acts after the work of clearing up the work of war contracts was completed. This statement totaled, under armament of fortifications, continental United States, $786,264,146.97; armament of fortifications, insular possessions, $5,077,699.58; and armament of fortifications, Panama Canal, $2,306,481.73, or altogether, $793,648,328.28. These figures were arrived at by making a careful survey of expected expenditures for current orders, for existing portions of old war contracts, and for the settlement of claims, and other miscellaneous items. A great deal of time was spent and careful attention given to preparing the figures as to expected expenditures, and it is still believed that our estimates are approximately correct. The totals of these expected expenditures by each appropriation were subtracted from the Treasury balances, and the differences thereof were the amounts expected to be surplus under each appropriation. The Treasury balances were obtained from the Director of Finance, as the Ordnance Office has no means of ascertaining these balances from its own books. Since submitting that statement to the House committee information has been received from the Director of Finance that the figures furnished the Ordnance Department of the Treasury balance under armament of fortifications, continental United States, were too great by $191,-870,000. Consequently the expected surplus under armament of fortifications, continental United States, was too great by that amount and can not possibly exceed $594,394,146.97.

Maj. BROWN. Col. Gatchell, will you permit me to say a word there in corroboration of your statement? I am speaking for the Director of Finance with regard to that change in the figures furnished by the Director of Finance.

Senator SMOOT. Right there, tell me what should be the amount of armament of fortifications? The House provides that there shall be turned back $786,264,146.97.

Col. GATCHELL. Yes, sir.

Senator SMOOT. What do you claim?

Col. GATCHELL. This reduction would reduce it to $594,394,146.97.

Senator SMOOT. Fortifications in insular possessions, how much?

Col. RICE. We do not consider it safe to turn in that amount of money.

Col. GATCHELL. We wish to make a plea not to turn in more than $500,000,000.

Senator SMOOT. Do you mean on all three items?

Col. RICE. Yes, sir.

Col. GATCHELL. I was going to substantiate that statement with what we wish to do.

Senator SMOOT. I want each item. You have given me armament of fortifications. Now, under fortifications in insular possessions you turn back $5,077,699.58. What should it be?

Col. GATCHELL. We do not wish to turn in any under that.

Senator SMOOT. Nothing at all?

Col. RICE. There is $500,000,000 under continental armament of fortifications and nothing under the others.

Col. GATCHELL. I should like to submit a statement as to the reasons.

Senator SMOOT. Now, under "Armament of Fortifications, Panama Canal," there is $2,306,481.73. What do you want?

Col. GATCHELL. We desire not to turn in any of that, sir.

Senator SMOOT. You had better tell us why.

Col. GATCHELL. Yes, sir. Whereas this surplus is expected when all the old work is completed, this money is not available to be turned into the Treasury at the present time, and if returned to the surplus fund would create artificial deficits in the Ordnance Department accounts. Briefly, some of this money is still allotted, and should not be revoked as yet. There are hundreds of allotments in the hands of disbursing officers, and it is impossible for the disbursing officers to compute accurately just how much money will be needed under each allotment, although they are able to make a general survey of the situation and approximate very closely how much money will be needed by their offices in total. So very properly, in reporting funds for revocation, they are necessarily keeping a margin in each allotment to meet unforeseen contingencies, and to prevent numerous difficulties in reallotting them money should such necessity arise.

The Ordnance Department has conducted a vigorous campaign to obtain as large a free balance as possible and, as a result of this work, there is a free balance and can be returned to the surplus fund of the Treasury at the present time $500,000,000 under "Armament of Fortifications, Continental United States," and it is desired that the fortifications bill, as passed by the House of Representatives, be amended by striking out, on page 16, line 20, the figures "$786,264,-146.97" and substituting therefor "$500,000,000."

With reference to the amounts expected to be surplus under "Insular possessions and Panama Canal appropriations," owing to the difficulty of communicating promptly with the disbursing officers in

Panama, Hawaii, and the Philippines, it is earnestly requested that none of these funds be declared surplus at this time. The amount involved is comparatively small, only totaling slightly over $7,-000,000, and if the money were returned at this time, it is believed that the margin is too small to risk not having money to meet obligations already incurred. It is, therefore, requested that, on page 16, line 23, the figures "$5,077,699.58" be stricken out and "$628,784.17" substituted therefor, which, it is understood, applies to appropriations for the Engineer Corps. This has been verified by reference to the office of the Chief of Engineers.

Also, on page 17, lines 2 and 3, the words and figures "armament of fortifications, Panama Canal, $2,306,481.73" should be stricken out. Of course, if these amendments are adopted as requested, the total, as shown on page 17, line 7, would have to be reduced accordingly.

It is to be noted that with these corrections the Ordnance Department is turning in five-sixths of its total expected surplus, but desires to retain the remaining one-sixth.

Senator OVERMAN. How much will that reduce it? The total here is $800,000,000.

Col. GATCHELL. I had those figures here. I will look for them.

Senator OVERMAN. Never mind; we can get it.

Col. RICE. Approximately $300,000,000, including the error of about $200,000,000.

Senator OVERMAN. I will not detain you. Go ahead.

Col. GATCHELL. We want to retain one-sixth, in order to prevent numerous difficulties which would arise if the entire total were recovered to the Treasury now, but which will not occur if only the amount recommended is so recovered. Furthermore, it is believed that with the huge amount of work involved, it leaves the Ordnance Department with a reasonable working balance and obviates all possibility of necessity for deficiency appropriations to meet obligations which might arise if the entire estimated amount is turned in. In other words, the figures recommended are known to be clear and free, whereas the total is an estimate only and may vary considerably.

The amendments requested are urgently recommended.

I might add, Mr. Chairman, that in our testimony before the House committee we only had at that time about $256,000,000 free, and that was the amount that we stated as free and which we were willing to turn in. The other was a statement of what we expected to have when we got through—a statement which Mr. Slemp, the chairman of the subcommittee, asked for—but we never at any time expressed ourselves as willing to turn in that money now.

Senator SMOOT. It is not a question as to whether you are willing to do it. It is a question as to whether we can do it and appropriate as the needs arise.

Col. GATCHELL. We do not believe it would be safe to do it.

Senator SMOOT. I do not believe in the policy of the past of piling these things up and having an unexpended balance in the Treasury of the United States to be dealt with as the department pleases. I want the amount of money appropriated that will be expended within the year and no more, and let the department come to Congress every year and tell Congress what is going to be done with it.

Col. GATCHELL. This money, under the provisions of the fortifications act of last year, ceases to be available for obligations on July 1 of this year anyway; and the Ordnance Department, as you know, of course has no intention to making any new obligations other than are absolutely necessary.

In preparing the original estimated surplus, expected new obligations were taken into account.

At the time this estimate was prepared the Ordnance Department had obligations to pay under—

Outstanding claims and unpaid awards	$145, 343, 421. 01
Balances due on old contracts	83, 875, 475. 25
Estimated expenditures on current orders	45, 254, 139. 95
Miscellaneous maintenance items for remainder of fiscal year	22, 924, 608. 01
Total	297, 397, 644. 22

The Treasury balance on January 15, 1920, which was used as a basis in preparing this estimate, was reported to the Ordnance Department as $1,083,661,791.19. This should be reduced by the $191,870,000 error in the Treasury balance previously referred to, leaving the correct Treasury balance $891,791,791.19. If the $786,264,146.97 be recovered to the Treasury Department, as provided in the bill as passed by the House of Representatives, the Ordnance Department would have only $105,527,644.22 to meet outstanding obligations amounting to practically $300,000,000.

The Ordnance Department has free on its books to-day approximately $500,000,000 under the appropriation titles contained in this bill. The remaining $94,000,000 which it is estimated can be eventually recovered to the Treasury Department is now in the hands of disbursing officers in the form of allotments covering old war contracts. The amount of money which they actually have is, of course, much greater than this, but this is the amount which it is expected they will not spend but will eventually revoke from their allotments. The amount is made up of estimates submitted by these disbursing officers, but, as previously stated, it is not possible for them to definitely determine how much shall come from each allotment, and therefore it is not possible to make the revocations at this time. The revocations will be made as rapidly as the contracts are cleaned up. However, it is wished to emphasize the fact that whereas $500,000,000 is a known, definite figure, the remaining $94,000,000 is purely and simply an estimate and may vary considerably one way or the other. The Ordnance Department, therefore, does not deem it safe at the present time to recover more than $500,000,000.

Senator OVERMAN. Do you mean to say that all these appropriations are for obligations that are outstanding?

Col. GATCHELL. All this money ceases to be available for obligations on July 1.

Senator OVERMAN. Have you obligations outstanding to cover this amount?

Col. GATCHELL. No, sir.

Senator SMOOT. No; they can be made up until July 1.

Senator OVERMAN. I understand that, but I wanted to know whether he meant that the obligations were new obligations.

Col. GATCHELL. No, sir. We feel that this money will be free when we finish. The point is this: That money is out in the hands of disbursing officers, other than about $500,000,000, which we are ready and perfectly willing to turn in; but the other money, the difference between that and the $594,000,000, is now in the hands of disbursing officers in the form of allotments under old contracts which are being settled by claim, and which involve various difficulties, so that it would put us in a very embarrassing situation if this money were turned in and we had to revoke those allotments to get the money to turn in. Then we would have to reallot, and it would cause a great deal of trouble and difficulty.

Col. RICE. It is a matter of closing out the war payments.

Senator SMOOT. Suppose we reduce this $300,000,000, as you are asking us to do: By July 1 of this year would you enter into obligations covering that full amount?

Col. RICE. No, sir.

Col. GATCHELL. No, sir. We have no idea of entering into such new obligations.

Senator SMOOT. Then, if you do not want to do that, why do you want it to remain in the fund?

Col. GATCHELL. The money is out under obligations at the present time. We expect to be able to revoke those obligations. When they are closed and settled, there will be certain money left under those allotments which can be revoked and at that time turned into the Treasury.

Senator SMOOT. You do not want us to do it at this time?

Col. GATCHELL. No, sir. There is $200,000,000 of this which must be reduced because of the error in the Treasury balance which was furnished us. That was beyond our power altogether. We had nothing to do with that. The only thing that we are asking for as a privilege to the Ordnance Department is to retain $100,000,000.

Senator SMOOT. You have reference to the $191,870,000 that was an error in the figures of the Finance Service?

Col. GATCHELL. Yes, sir.

Maj. BROWN. May I say a word as to that; sir?

Senator SMOOT. Yes, sir.

Maj. BROWN. I am from the Finance Service. I wish to say that Col. Gatchell is correct in making the statement that the incorrect figures were furnished by the Office of the Director of Finance.

Senator SMOOTH. How did it happen?

Maj. BROWN. Gen. Lord asked me to make this statement frankly to the committee, in justice to the Ordnance Department, and to state further that the original error from which it grew was made by the personnel—the ordnance officer and ordnance civilian personnel—which were transferred to the Office of the Director of Finance at the time of the consolidation of finance.

I should like to say, in explanation of that, that when the Finance Service was created in 1918 it was, of course, made up of personnel transferred from the other bureaus, along with the funds which were transferred. There was a maze of appropriations, contract authorizations, etc., which was rather complicated. The personnel transferred with that was made up of emergency officers and temporary employees, many of them of quite considerable efficiency, and they alone were familiar with those appropriations and the situation with regard to them. Obviously, the correct procedure was to leave them to handle the books in connection with the appropriations. That was done; and this is, of course, no reflection whatever on the Ordnance Department as it is at present, but simply a statement of the conditions as they exist. The funds were necessarily handled by temporary personnel.

Senator SMOOT. Was this information presented to the House?

Maj. BROWN. What I am stating now, or the figures?

Senator SMOOT. What you are stating now.

Maj. BROWN. We discovered the error after the statement was presented to the House and after the bill had been passed by the House; in fact, it has just been discovered. Immediately on its discovery, we notified the Ordnance Department.

Senator SMOOT. Col. Gatchell, have you anything else to say?

Col. RICE. I should like simply to put in the record the statement that the error seems to us to have been made due to a change in the system of bookkeeping rather than anything else, but I do not think that feature is important.

Senator SMOOT. No; not if you can get the $191,000,000.

Col. GATCHELL. No.

Maj. BROWN. It is a question of fact. The money simply is not there.

Col. RICE. That is all we have, sir.

Senator SMOOT. Thank you.

Col. RICE. Thank you for your courtesy.

STATEMENT OF MAJ. GEN. F. W. COE, UNITED STATES ARMY, CHIEF OF COAST ARTILLERY.

FIRE CONTROL AT FORTIFICATIONS.

Senator SMOOT. Gen. Coe, on what part of the bill do you desire to be heard?

Gen. COE. Mr. Chairman, only on two items on page 16, section 8. The first is in line 18, covering back into the Treasury an item of $1,376,008 from the appropriation for fire-control at fortifications. I should like to have that amount reduced to $975,075.72, which is the present Treasury balance, and which is immediately available for return upon the passage of the bill.

Senator SMOOT. How did the House come to include the full amount of $1,376,008?

Gen. COE. They came to that figure by reason of the statement which we made that we expected to have that balance available to turn in on June 30, and we still expect to have that balance; but in accordance with the testimony previously given, the difference between the two amounts is now allotted and in the hands of various district officers, and to withdraw it until their accounts are settled on June 30 will make a difficulty. They know that they have to have their accounts settled on June 30, and that all unexpended balances at that time revert to the Treasury; but to draw that in at the present time would result in considerable difficulty, especially with the Engineer Department. We do not expect to enter into any obligations—it is not for that purpose that we ask that this reduction be made—but simply that the difference between those two amounts may remain available until the 30th of June.

Senator OVERMAN. You say this money will go back after the 30th of June?

Gen. COE. Yes, sir.

Senator OVERMAN. This bill does not go into effect until that time.

Gen. COE. Yes, sir; but this item goes into effect upon the passage of the bill.

Senator OVERMAN. It does?

Senator SMOOT. Upon the approval of the act.

Senator OVERMAN. Oh, yes; I see—upon the approval of the act.

Gen. COE. We have now in the Treasury the amount stated, $975,075.72, and we have no use for that. The remainder is allotted, and we probably will save about that amount.

CONTINGENT EXPENSES, SEACOAST FORTIFICATIONS.

The other item for which I would ask a reduction is on line 17, Contingent Expenses, Seacoast Fortifications. The amount directed to be revoked is $49,985.36.

Senator SMOOT. What do you want it reduced to?

Gen. COE. I should like to have that reduced to zero. During the period while the hearings were going on, due to action taken upon recommendations made prior to the hearings, the actual Treasury balance has already been reduced in that case to $18,948.88; but we may need that for various emergencies which may come up at any time between now and the 30th of June. I should like to have that amount reduced to zero, so as to leave us the $18,948.88 which we still have for any emergency that may arise.

Those are the only items to which I have to call attention.

STATEMENT OF COL. C. O. SHERRILL, UNITED STATES ARMY, IN CHARGE OF FORTIFICATIONS, OFFICE OF CHIEF OF ENGINEERS.

MODERNIZING OF OLDER EMPLACEMENTS.

Senator SMOOT. What part of the bill do you desire to be heard on?

Col. SHERRILL. The beginning of the bill, page 2, line 5. It is requested that the item of $37,250 be changed to read " $120,295." This is the item that was reported to the House Appropriations Committee as absolutely essential, and an item of approximately $37,250 was reported as necessary but not essential. In making the recommendations, the smaller sum of $37,250 was granted. Subsequently to the hearings before the Appropriations Committee the War Department called a conference at which all the different services were present and all of the different items were carefully examined, and the items that we are now presenting were agreed upon by the War Department and the different services as absolutely essential for proper operation of the work.

Senator SMOOT. What is the next item?

PRESERVATION AND REPAIR OF FORTIFICATIONS.

Col. SHERRILL. The next item is found on line 10 of the same page. It is requested that " $300,000 " in line 10 be increased to " $400,000."

Senator SMOOT. That was the estimate?

Col. SHERRILL. Yes, sir; for the same reason.

CONSTRUCTION OF FIRE-CONTROL STATION.

On page 3, line 23 (Senate print, page 3, line 24), it is requested that the words " not to exceed $48,755 for the " be stricken out. The reason for making that request is that that is new legislation, in that heretofore we have had general authority to purchase small sites for fire-control stations not involving large sums or large amounts of land, but as the necessity for small stations arose we have been allowed to make those purchases.

The reason why that was inserted by the Appropriations Committee was that when the hearing was held it was stated to them that land in the approximate amount of the sum which is indicated here had already been purchased, but payment could not be made on account of the prohibition in the Army act of last year forbidding such payments. For that reason, this amount was considerably stressed, and the committee in using that figure stated that sums in excess of that could not be used. That would practically nullify this entire appropriation or a large part of this appropriation for fire control, because we could not buy any of the small sites that are necessary for that purpose.

There is no intention to buy more than the minimum essential land, and that comes in for these isolated stations usually in small tracts of an acre, or a half acre, or something like that. It is not any project for buying large amounts of land, but it is very essential, in order to get this work done, that that provision be stricken out. That will leave just the same language that has always been in the bill.

LAND DEFENSES, HAWAIIAN ISLANDS.

The next item is page 8, line 13, where we desire to have the figures " $130,000 " changed to " $560,000."

Senator SMOOT. You want the estimate. We have a letter in regard to that already.

Col. SHERRILL. Yes, sir.

Senator SMOOT. You need not go into the details. The letter covers that.

Col. SHERRILL. Yes, sir.

PROCUREMENT OF LAND FOR FORTIFICATIONS, HAWAIIAN ISLANDS.

On the same page, line 17, I should like to increase the estimate of $25,760 to $205,760. That item is to provide a site for armament on the north shore of the Island of Oahu, which has been strongly recommended by the War Department, and the War Department has directed the Chief of Engineers to resubmit that with the request that it be granted. The details of that are found in the other hearings.

PLANS FOR FORTIFICATIONS, HAWAIIAN ISLANDS.

The next item is on page 8, line 19, where we desire to have the words " Philippine Islands " changed to " Hawaiian Islands." The

House subcommittee was requested to allow $3,000 for plans for the Hawaiian Islands, and to drop the item of $3,000 for the Philippine Islands.

Senator SMOOT. You requested $3,000 for the Philippine Islands and $3,000 for the Hawaiian Islands?

Col. SHERRILL. Yes, sir; but we stated that the one for the Philippine Islands might be dropped, probably, and an error was made by which we were given this for the Philippines instead of Hawaii. That is just to make that correction.

Senator OVERMAN. It is more important to have it at Hawaii than it is at the Philippines?

Col. SHERRILL. Yes, sir; because we are doing more work there. It is a more important place.

SEA WALLS AND EMBANKMENT, PANAMA CANAL.

The next item is on page 12, following line 8. It is recommended that the following wording be inserted:

For the construction of sea walls and embankments, $500,000.

That was carried in the estimate. There are present to defend this estimate representatives of the Navy Department, in whose interest, largely, this was inserted in the bill. That is, both the War and Navy Departments are vitally interested in this item. The views of the War Department have already been presented, and I request that the naval officers present be given an opportunity to state why it is necessary for the Navy.

STATEMENT OF CAPT. H. V. BUTLER, UNITED STATES NAVY, FROM OFFICE OF THE CHIEF OF NAVAL OPERATIONS.

Capt. BUTLER. Mr. Chairman, this item is to close the gap between the present east breakwater and Margarita Point at the Atlantic entrance to the Panama Canal, first, for the purpose of protecting the submarine base and the aviation station belonging to the Government at Coco Solo Point; second, to form a protected anchorage there, with smooth water, for such auxiliary vessels as may be there to serve the two bases; and, third, to form a smooth-water place for the Navy seaplanes to take off from.

First, the protection is needed against the trade winds, which blow from the north and northeast for about six months in the spring and early summer, and from the severe northers which blow during the winter practically from October to April. The winds themselves are not so strong, but they pile up the water. On account of the heavy swells that come in from the ocean and sweep in around the point there, we are in danger if having damage done to the bases for the submarines and aircraft.

The forming of a protected harbor is, first, for the protection of smaller vessels of the fleet that might anchor there, but more particularly those auxiliaries which would serve these two bases; second, for small boating from vessels anchored there into the bases, and, third, and really the most important part, forming a smooth-water body wherefrom the seaplanes can take off. At the present time we are having considerable damage done to our seaplanes there in ordinary, moderate weather. In time of storms, in which, of course, we would have to operate in war time, it would be impossible for those planes to take off there.

Senator SMOOT. What is the total estimated cost of this project?

Capt. BUTLER. One million eight hundred thousand dollars.

Senator SMOOT. You are asking $500,000 to begin the project?

Capt. BUTLER. Yes, sir; this year.

Senator SMOOT. I notice that Col. Sherrill gave detailed testimony upon this subject before the House committee. If there is not anything special outside of his testimony there is no need of taking any further time, because we are going to consider this testimony as given in the House.

Capt. BUTLER. Yes, sir. That is all I have to say, Mr. Chairman.

CONTINUATION OF STATEMENT OF COL. C. O. SHERRILL, UNITED STATES ARMY, IN CHARGE OF FORTIFICATIONS, OFFICE OF CHIEF OF ENGINEERS.

PLANS FOR FORTIFICATIONS, PANAMA CANAL.

Col. SHERRILL. The next item is on page 12, following the item that we have just discussed, where we request the insertion of the following:

For preparation of plans for fortifications and other works of defense, including surveys for roads, $50,000.

Senator OVERMAN. That is in the Canal Zone?

Col. SHERRILL. Yes, sir. That has been given in detail; but, as I said before, the War Department is extremely anxious to have this in order that we can get up a plan of defense for the Panama Canal.

EMPLOYMENT OF SERVICES IN THE DISTRICT OF COLUMBIA.

The next item is page 16, line 5, where it is requested that the following be added:

Provided, That the services of skilled draftsmen, civil engineers, and such other services as the Secretary of War may deem necessary may be employed only in the office of the Chief of Engineers to carry into effect the various appropriations for " Engineer equipment of troops," " Engineer operations in the field." and other military operations, to be paid from such appropriations: and the legislative, executive, and judicial act for the fiscal year 1921 is amended accordingly: *Provided further,* That the expenditures on this account for the fiscal year 1921 shall not exceed $100,000.

Senator SMOOT. That means that you want $100,000 to be expended in Washington?

Col. SHERRILL. No, sir; the point is we wish to be authorized to use field funds which are appropriated elsewhere to that extent, in order that the development work to be carried on can be effectively carried on, which must be done in Washington.

Senator SMOOT. The amendment you want is to the effect that $100,000 of the appropriation may be expended in Washington instead of in the field?

Col. SHERRILL. Yes, sir: and that is absolutely vital, because this is the only place where we can get conferences with the different War Department authorities necessary for that development work. It can not be done effectively nor economically in any other place.

SUPPLIES FOR SEACOAST DEFENSES.

The next item is on page 16, following line 12:

Supplies for seacoast defenses, $40,000.

That is a revocation which is not included in the act. We find that we can turn in that additional sum of money.

Senator OVERMAN. What line is that?

Col. SHERRILL. Following line 12, on page 16.

Senator SMOOT. What is the language?

Col. SHERRILL. "Supplies for seacoast defenses, $40,000."

Senator SMOOT. All right.

SITES FOR FORTIFICATIONS, ETC.

Col. SHERRILL. Line 13, strike out " $63,346.68 " and in lieu thereof insert " $88,292.88." We are turning in there a larger sum than we contemplated. With further knowledge we find that we are able to turn in more money.

ELECTRICAL AND SOUND-RANGING EQUIPMENT.

Line 15, strike out " $2,260,050.69 " and insert in lieu thereof " $2,073,881.96." That, Mr. Chairman, does not mean that we are going to spend any more money, but it means that we have further information which indicates that that is the total that we will be able to turn in. It would lapse in any case on the 30th of June, and a letter has been written with reference to that matter.

FORTIFICATIONS IN INSULAR POSSESSIONS.

The next item is in line 23. There were some new figures given there by the Ordnance Department; " $628,784.17 " should be stricken out and " $731,234.17 " inserted.

Senator SMOOT. Line 23, you say?

Maj. BROWNE. That item, as it appears in the House bill, namely, $5,077,699.58, is made up of both ordnance and engineer items.

Senator SMOOT. Oh, I see. What did you say you wanted?

Col. SHERRILL. The Ordnance Department struck out the item that now appears and put in " $628,784.17 " as being the amount the Engineer Department was expected to turn in. We wish to amend that, and turn in still further to the total extent of $731,234.17. We find we can turn in more money.

Senator SMOOT. The difference is between the amount that Col. Gatchell reported and what you find you can turn in?

Col. SHERRILL. Yes, sir; we can turn in more money than we thought.

FUNDS FOR WORK UNDER ENGINEER DEPARTMENT.

On that same page, Mr. Chairman, I failed to give one provision of new legislation which we request to go in after line 5, as section 8:

That all funds appropriated herein that are applied to work carried out under the Engineer Department shall remain available until December 31, 1921.

That matter was explained before the House Appropriations Com- mittee where it asked that funds be made available for two fiscal years, and it seemed necessary on account of construction work being done by day labor in order to avoid additional expense due to break- ing up the work in the middle of the season. The House having failed to grant the original request, an extension of only six months is now being urged. It does not involve any additional expenditure, but makes it more economical in administration, and the Chief of Engineers requests very strongly that that be inserted.

Senator SMOOT. That date is December 31, 1921?

Col. SHERRILL. Yes, sir; six months longer, in other words, so that it will cover one full working season without breaking into the middle of it.

SUBMARINE MINE STRUCTURES.

On page 17, after line 1, insert:

Submarine mine structures, $15,200.

That is an additional sum to be turned in.

I wish to call attention to the fact that the Engineer Department is turning in under these proposed changes almost as much as it did before. The only large item in which we are asking to have less turned in is under the item for electrical and sound-ranging equip- ment, in which we ask a decrease in the amount to be withdrawn; but in a number of other items we report an increase, so it largely balances.

There is one other insertion I request to be made. That is on page 12, following line 6:

SEARCHLIGHTS FOR PANAMA CANAL FORTIFICATIONS.

For the purchase and installation of searchlights for the seacoast fortifica- tions on the Canal Zone, $6,000.

That, Mr. Chairman, is an item for completing the searchlight system of the Canal Zone, and it is considered highly essential that it be granted. It provides for building some concrete operating platforms to take the place of decayed and rotten wooden ones. It is essential for the operation of the searchlights.

That covers all the items that the Chief of Engineers has to present.

STATEMENT OF MAJ. JOHN J. KINGMAN, GENERAL STAFF, UNITED STATES ARMY.

MILITARY ROADS, OAHU ISLAND.

Maj. KINGMAN. There is one item which Col. Sherrill has already spoken of upon which the War Plans Division wishes to lay em- phasis, and that is the item for military roads in Oahu—page 8, line 13. It is covered there under the heading of "Land defenses." This I have discussed in a paper here, Mr. Chairman, which I should like to have included in the record.

Senator SMOOT. Hand it to the stenographer.

(The paper is as follows:)

WAR DEPARTMENT,
OFFICE OF THE CHIEF OF STAFF,
Washington, April 22, 1920.

Memorandum.

Subject: Military roads on Oahu.

1. The first plans prepared by the Army for defending the naval base at Pearl Harbor contemplated merely defending a line of hills quite close to Pearl Harbor. Subsequent studies and our experience during the World War have convinced us that a positive defense of this vitally important naval base must provide for defending the entire island of Oahu by preventing an enemy landing at any point on the coast. The recently revised plan of the department commander contemplates this system of defense. It necessitates that our garrison shall be able to concentrate rapidly at any point on the coast where the enemy may attempt to land. He is weakest at this time, but if he be permitted to get a considerable force on shore our chances of defeating him grow steadily less and the capture of the island becomes only a matter of time, if the enemy has command of the sea. The garrison has been centrally located at Schofield Barracks, and from there it must be able to move rapidly with infantry, artillery, machine guns, tanks, ammunition wagons, etc., to any threatened point on the coast. This means that we must have a suitable system of roads radiating from Schofield Barracks.

2. It is very desirable, of course, from a Federal standpoint, that as much as possible of this road work be paid for by the local authorities. It has, however, been definitely determined that the local authorities will not build all of the roads necessary for military purposes, because some of these roads are not necessary to the local population. All of the roads built by the Territory will be useful to the Army garrison, and no doubt some of the roads to be built by the Army will be used to some extent by the civil populattion.

3. In a report dated December 27, 1919, the commanding general Hawaiian Department submitted a revised project for military roads on Oahu, the total cost of which to the War Department would be $4,814,000 and to the Navy Department $85,000. In this new project the necessary roads are divided into three classes:

Class I includes those roads which are necessary merely for military reasons. The entire expense of building and maintaining Class I roads is to be borne by the Federal Government.

Class II roads are to be constructed and maintained by the local authorities except that the Federal Government is to build and maintain the bridges and culverts. This expense to the Federal Government appears necessary in order to secure bridges and culverts of capacity sufficient to carry the heavy guns, tractors, etc., necessary in the defense of the island.

Class III roads are to be built and maintained entirely by the local authorities.

4. The original fortifications appropriation bill, 1921, contained an item of $500,000 to initiate work upon this road project, but most of it was omitted from the bill as passed by the House. It is now strongly urged that this item be reinserted by the Senate.

The construction of these roads on Oahu is not only vitally important to the national defense but the need for an appropriation is urgent. as much time will be required to complete the work. The naval base at Pearl Harbor is the most important of all our bases in the Pacific and, moreover, its protection in the event of a serious war is the most critical element of the national defense. By this it is meant that, if strongly defended, the island can probably be held, but otherwise it would likely be lost during a war in which we were unable to maintain a naval superiority in the Pacific.

JOHN J. KINGMAN,
Major, General Staff.

Maj. KINGMAN. The War Plans Division considers this question of military roads as being one of the very most important items covered in the entire bill.

STATEMENT OF MAJ. GEN. CHARLES T. MENOHER, UNITED STATES ARMY, DIRECTOR OF AIR SERVICE.

AIR SERVICE.

Gen. MENOHER. Mr. Chairman, I should like to make a brief general statement in regard to the estimates that we desire to have considered, and then I can submit more detailed figures to go in the record.

Senator SMOOT. What page and line do you refer to?

Gen. MENOHER. Page 4, after line 17.

Senator OVERMAN. Under what item is it?

Gen. MENOHER. Air Service.

Senator OVERMAN. That is not on line 4.

Gen. MENOHER. We are asking only for a continuation of funds, not for any new appropriation, for the first project that I have in mind—that is, continental United States.

Senator HARRIS. General, what page and what line are you on there?

Maj. BROWN. He is asking for the insertion of language that is not in the bill before you, to come in on page 7, right after " Barracks and quarters."

Col. A. L. FULLER. The reference is to the printed bill here as passed by the House, and it follows the item " Under the Chief Signal Officer," on page 4 of this print.

Senator SMOOT. That is following line 16, page 4. It does not make any difference, I suppose, where it comes in. Now, what do you want to insert there?

Gen. MENOHER. The insert desired is as follows:

AIR SERVICE.

For the establishment, construction, enlargement, or improvement of aviation stations for use in connection with the seacoast defenses of the continental United States the unexpended balances of the appropriations contained in the act approved February 14, 1917, and in the act approved July 8, 1918, for aviation purposes are hereby made available until June 30, 1921 : *Provided*, That the Secretary of War is authorized to expend of this amount $596,725, or so much thereof as may be necessary, for the purchase or acquisition of land necessary for aviation stations in connection with these coast defenses : *Provided further*, That in the establishment of these stations the following limits of cost of structures are authorized but shall not be exceeded : For each acre repair shop $76,010, for each storehouse and guardhouse $20,952, for each combined administration building, radio, photographic, and fire house $53,544, for each hospital building $34,920, for each field officers' quarters $15,000, for each company officers' quarters $12,000, for each barracks $110,000, for each boathouse and dock $55,972.

Senator SMOOT. I will say that the committee has received a letter from the Secretary of War, dated April 18, 1920, covering this subject; and unless there is something that you particularly want to call attention to that is not contained in that letter, I will state that the committee has the matter now before it.

Gen. MENOHER. Yes, sir. I beg to ask the committee to keep in mind the fact that we are asking for no new appropriation. We have not asked for any. We have asked for a continuation of funds that have already been appropriated in 1917 and 1918, $11,600,000, and there remains an unobligated balance of those funds, and unexpended balance, that we desire to be continued in order that we may carry on to completion the work that has been authorized by Congress.

Senator SMOOT. What amount?

Gen. MENOHER. There is $6,710,490.38 still remaining unobligated that we want to have continued. Then that is further increased so that the grand total that we desire to have continued is $9,617,179.38.

As I say, this was for the construction of eight aerial stations for use in connection with the seacoast defenses within the United States. Sixteen were decided upon as being of importance. Eight of the more important were selected for completion first, and for which the funds referred to were appropriated by Congress. They all have to do with the seacoast defenses of the United States, a purely defensive proposition. They are auxiliary to the seacoast defenses and necessary to carrying out observation, spotting, etc., of the defenses that are already in existence. So that we are not asking for any new appropriation, but only continuation of these balances, part of which—$3,600,000—was appropriated before the recent war.

Now, the reason that this work could not be carried on to completion was that we wanted to give further study to some of the projects. In the last appropriation bill there were provisions for the purchase of land, a number of the projects involving the purchase of land, in one case for the balloon base line in Narragansett Bay, or two balloons, forming the base line, and the purchase of land in five other places for the establishment of operation stations for the airplane projects at those places. Those are all laid out and given in detail in the hearings that we had before the House Military Committee. The House committee allowed us nothing for these projects in the continental United States. We would like to have that appropriation continued if possible.

We took this matter up again with the War Plans Division of the General Staff after the House bill had passed, and it was agreed in conference there that we should ask the Senate committee to continue these appropriations as being necessary to carry on the defense project of the continental United States.

Now, we are in process of obligating a part of this—about $3,000,000 of it. In fact, some of this amount has already been obligated. There is difficulty in doing this construction work in the short time we have had, because bids have been asked for and bids have been rejected and new ones asked for; and there is a question always whether we can obligate the balance before the 30th of June. In any event, it is proposed to go on with the stations at Staten Island, San Francisco, and Chesapeake Bay, and the balloon-base lines.

Senator SMOOT. Has that been covered in this letter?

Gen. MENOHER. It was covered in the House Military Committee, and in the letter from the Secretary of War in a more general way.

The next amendment has to do with the unexpended balance for our insular possessions. We ask for no new appropriations in the Philippines.

Senator SMOOT. What page?

Gen. Menoher. Page 11, line 14. Strike out the period at the end of the line and insert a colon followed by:

Provided, That the unexpended balances of the appropriations made for aviation purposes in connection with the seacoast defenses in the insular possessions in the act approved February 14, 1917, are hereby made available until June 30, 1921: *Provided further,* That in the establishment of these stations the following limits of cost of structures are authorized but shall not be exceeded: For each barracks, $40,000; for each post exchange, $30,000; for each seaplane hangar, $87,000; for each repair shop, $30,000; for each boathouse and dock, $24,000.

We ask for no new appropriation for the Philippines at all. We have an unallotted balance there of about $68,000, which is in process of being obligated, but we ran across the same thing there that we did in the United States, that in the time between now and June 30 we are very sure that it is difficult, on account of the great distance, to get definite and accurate reports.

Senator Smoot. I have a letter from the Secretary on that.

Gen. Menoher. That is one reason why we want this continued. It is a question as to whether we shall be able to obligate it before the 30th. If we are not able to obligate it, it might leave the work partially completed so that it would have to be held up and destruction and loss would necessarily result from that.

In regard to Oahu, the House Military Committee allowed us $1,300,000. That was a new appropriation, and they provided for covering into the Treasury our unobligated balance there of $302,000. Now, we would like to have that $302,000 continued in addition to the $1,300,000 that was provided for by new appropriation by the House committee.

Senator Smoot. $302,000?

Gen. Menoher. Yes, sir; that is in process of being obligated also; and the same thing may occur if we can not continue that on, and I believe the House bill provides that that shall be covered into the Treasury on the date of the passage of the act; so it will be no longer available after the passage of the act, and that would stop work right on that date. We would have to comply with that and stop work at that time. Special attention is invited to the proposed amendment covering limits of cost of structures. We must have this amendment so as to spend the $1,300,000 which the House gave us.

What we are estimating for provides only for the units that are over on the islands at present or are actually en route—that is, to complete the project as approved by the study of the authorities actually on the ground.

The only other item that we want to cover is the Panama Canal, and that is covered in a general way in the letter that the Secretary of War has sent to the committee.

This is an amendment to page 13. Strike out lines 11 to 25 and insert:

For the establishment, construction, enlargement, or improvement of aviation stations in the Canal Zone for use in connection with the seacoast defenses of Panama Canal, including the acquisition of land or any interest in land, by purchase, lease, condemnation, or otherwise, and the preparation necessary to make the same suitable for the purpose intended and for the acquisition and improvement of emergency land fields in Canal Zone, $2,730,793: *Provided,*

That in the construction herein appropriated for the following limits of cost of structures are authorized, but shall not be exceeded: For each barracks, $70,000; for each combination administration building, post exchange, assembly hall, guardhouse, and infirmary, $60,000; for each balloon hangar, $50,000; for each field-officers' quarters, $20,000; for each company-officers' quarters, $11,000.

The House provided for only $239,000 for the Panama Canal. We also took this matter up with the War Plans Division of the General Staff, and it was agreed that we should ask the Senate committee to give us about $2,700,000 for the Panama Canal, about $848,000 of that to be used for preparation of a landing field at the Pacific end of the canal. The exact amount asked for Panama is $2,738,793.

Senator OVERMAN. Is that included in this letter?

Gen. MENOHER. Yes; that is included. But what I want to invite attention to is the fact that there is no landing field on the Pacific end of the canal at all, and that facilities at that end are very inadequate, and we have lost lives on account of this lack of facilities. On the canal there are savannas within striking distance of the canal that could be used, with considerable preparation, for landing fields, and the initial cost of our proposition of grading the field at the Pacific end would be a little more than the preparation of a savanna. But considering the question of transportation out of these savannas as compared with that at the canal, I think in the end that the use of a savanna would be more expensive than this.

In case of war they would have to be prepared, perhaps, but this matter has been studied by the authorities on the ground and recommendations made in regard to the number of these places that might be available for landing fields, the Balboa field is the one that has their approval. It is the most feasible of all the projects proposed for a landing field at the Pacific end for the Canal Zone, and no matter what the final aerial defense of the Canal Zone will be, we must have this landing field at the Pacific end, and Balboa is the place where it should be, for, under all circumstances, an establishment will be required there.

Senator SMOOT. Is there anything further?

Gen. MENOHER. I have here to go into the record the detailed statement of the revised estimates as we want them. The Secretary of War's letter covers only the main items. This covers the estimates in detail of the revised project.

Senator SMOOT. It may go into the record.

(The estimates are here printed in the record as follows:)

ARMY AIR SERVICE, PANAMA PROJECT—SENATE REVISION.

PERSONNEL.

Present.—Total: 1 group headquarters, 1 observation squadron, 1 photo section; total, 19 officers and 173 men.

Proposed.—Total: 1 group headquarters, 10–59; 1 observation squadron, 47–210; 1 pursuit squadron, 32–202; 2 balloon companies, 16–340; total, 105 officers and 811 men.

France field.—1 observation group headquarters, 1 observation squadron, 1 photo section; total, 19 officers and 173 men; 1 observation group headquarters, 1 observation squadron, 1 pursuit squadron, hydroequipment; total, 89 officers and 471 men.

Fort Randolph.—1 balloon company; total, 8 officers and 170 men.

Fort Sherman.—1 balloon company; total, 8 officers and 170 men.

CONSTRUCTION.

In the following estimates concrete construction is intended for all principal buildings. Although frame construction would show a 25 per cent initial savings, experience has proven that this type of construction deteriorates very rapidly in the Canal Zone.

FRANCE FIELD PERSONNEL.

Present.—One group headquarters, 1 observation squadron, 1 photo section; total strength, 19 officers and 173 men.

Proposed.—One group headquarters, 1 observation squadron, 1 pursuit squadron, hydroequipment; 89 officers and 471 men.

	Revised estimate.
Barracks and quarters:	
2 field officers' quarters	$40,000
2 captains' quarters (2 officers each)	44,000
1 lieutenants' quarters (4 officers each)	30,000
3 unmarried officers' quarters (10 officers each set; total, 30 officers)	135,000
1 barracks for 200 men	70,000
Total	319,000
Technical buildings:	
Technical storehouse	15,000
Armory and dope, fabric, and radio-repair shop	16,000
Remodeling 11 seaplane hangars	75,000
Boathouse stalls (2 additional)	5,000
Total	111,000
General buildings:	
1 fire station	3,000
Special structures:	
Addition to garage	6,000
1 administration building (including post exchange, assembly hall, guardhouse, and 10-bed infirmary)	60,000
1 quartermaster's storehouse	18,000
Total	84,000
Utilities:	
Dry fill and grading around buildings	40,000
Street lighting	12,000
Municipal works	80,000
Addition to sea wall	35,000
Total	167,000
Preparation of flying fields:	
Extension of flying field	230,000
Emergency landing field	9,000
Total	239,000
For overhead and contingencies	167,935
Total	1,090,935

Recapitulation (France field).

Barracks and quarters	$319,000
Technical buildings	111,000
General buildings	3,000
Special structures	84,000
Utilities	167,000
Preparation of flying fields	239,000
For general overhead and contingencies	167,935
Total, revised estimate	1,090,935

Coco Solo (Fort Randolph), near France Field.

Personnel, proposed.—Eight officers, 170 men, 1 balloon company.

	Revised estimate.
2 captains' quarters	$22,000
1 set lieutenants' quarters (4 officers)	30,000
2 sets noncommissioned officers' quarters (8 N. C. O.s)	40,000
Barracks	70,000
Total	162,000
Storehouse	15,000
2 balloon sheds (42 by 100 by 40)	100,000
Total	115,000
Roads (3,750 feet)	35,750
Grading and fill	9,200
Walks	1,500
Water	11,250
Sewer	1,800
Electrical	17,000
Total	76,500
For overhead and contingencies	37,350
Total	390,850

Recapitulation (Coco Solo, Fort Randolph).

Barracks and quarters	162,000
Technical buildings	115,000
Utilities	76,500
For general overhead and contingencies	37,350
Total, revised estimate	390,850

Fort Sherman (Toro Point).

Personnel.—Present, none; proposed, 8 officers, 170 men, 1 balloon company.

	Revised estimate.
2 captains' quarters	$24,200
1 set lieutenant's quarters (4 officers)	33,000
2 sets noncommissioned quarters (8 N. C. O.)	44,000
1 barracks	77,000
Total	178,200
2 balloon sheds (42 by 100 by 40), frame	110,000
Storehouse	16,500
Garage	5,500
Total	126,500
Roads (2,000 feet)	14,000
Grading	2,800
Walks (1,600 square yards)	3,200
Water lines (1,800 feet)	4,200
Sewer (2,200 feet)	4,380
Sanitation, contiguous areas	6,800
Electrical	26,000
Total	61,380
For overhead and contingencies	37,128
Total	408,708

Recapitulation—Fort Sherman (Toro Point).

Barracks and quarters	$178, 200
Technical buildings	126, 500
Special structures	5, 500
Utilities	61, 380
For general overhead and contingencies	37, 128
Total revised estimate	408, 708

Pacific terminus of canal.

	Revised estimate.
Landing field, Pacific terminus:	
Grading fill	$128, 300
Dry fill	720, 000
Total	848, 300

Recapitulation—Panama fortifications, revised estimates fiscal year 1921, all projects—Senate revision.

Barracks and quarters	$659, 200
Technical buildings	352, 500
General buildings	3, 000
Special structures	89, 500
Utilities	304, 880
Preparation of flying fields	1, 087, 300
For general overhead and contingencies	242, 413
Grand total revised estimate as submitted	2, 738, 793

Army Air Service—Hawaiian project—Senate revision.

PERSONNEL.

Luke Field.—Present: One group headquarters, 2 observation squadrons—total, 35 officers, 310 men. Proposed: One group headquarters (10–59), 2 observation squadrons (94–420)—total, 104 officers, 479 men.

Fort Kamehameha.—Present: One balloon company (en route)—total, 8 officers, 170 men. Proposed: One balloon company—total, 8 officers, 170 men.

Fort Ruger.—Present: One balloon company (en route)—total, 8 officers, 170 men. Proposed: One balloon company—total, 8 officers, 170 men.

Total.—Present: One group headquarters, 2 observation squadrons, 2 balloon companies—total, 51 officers, 650 men. Proposed: One group headquarters, 2 observation squadrons, 2 balloon companies—total, 120 officers, 819 men.

CONSTRUCTION.

In the following revised estimates frame construction is intended for all buildings. This is in accordance with the adopted policy for construction in the Hawaiian Islands.

LUKE FIELD.

2 field officers' quarters	$18, 000	
20 married officers' quarters	160, 000	
32 bachelors' quarters (4 sets, 8 per set)	48, 000	
20 noncommissioned officers' quarters	60, 000	
2 barracks	80, 000	
		$366, 000
1 hospital	10, 000	
1 administration building	10, 000	
1 post exchange	20, 000	
1 fire station	3, 000	
1 guardhouse	10, 000	
1 laundry	3, 500	
1 bakery	5, 000	
		61, 500

2 sewage-disposal plants	$30.000	
12,000 feet sewer pipe	36,000	
		$66,000
3.000 feet main road, 30 feet wide	19,904	
1,800 feet main road. 24 feet wide	9,600	
6,450 feet quarters road, 20 feet wide	28,665	
5,100 feet service road, 16 feet wide	18,135	
2 miles sidewalk	10,000	
		86,304

Water supply:

10,000 square feet land, McGrews Peninsula	2,000	
5,000 feet flexible joint, 10-inch cast-iron pipe	18,750	
1,200 feet B. & S. 10-inch cast-iron pipe	3,420	
Plant for laying pipe	9,000	
Laying of flexible pipe	18,000	
1,200 feet B. & S. pipe	2,400	
		53,570

Pumping plant:

2 pump units	2,450	
Installing same	350	
1 Venturi meter and placing	1,500	
1 concrete pump house	4,800	
Power lines	1,100	
		10,200
10.000 water mains	32,000	
1 pressure and storage tank	11,000	
Cost of erection	2,000	
Fire hydrants	2,800	
		47,800
Street lighting		25,000
House lighting		
2 fuel storage		16,000
1 seaplane hangar		87,000
Total		819,374

FORT KAMEHAMEHA.

2 balloon hangars	$24,000	
1 storehouse	10,000	
1 repair hangar	12,000	
1 garage	6,500	
		$52,500
1 barracks	40,000	
1 field officers' quarters	9,000	
5 company officers' quarters	40,000	
4 noncommissioned officers' quarters	12,000	
		101,000
Walks		2,000
Roads		12,000
Water		6,000
Sewers		12,500
Light and power		5,000
Purchase land		105,000
Total		296,000
Contingencies		18,126
Grand total		314,126

FORT RUGER.

1 storehouse	$10,000	
1 garage	6,500	
		$16,500

1 barracks	$40,000
1 field officers' quarters	9,000
5 company officers' quarters	40,000
4 noncommissioned officers' quarters	12,000
	$101,000
Walks	3,000
Roads	9,000
Water	6,000
Sewers	9,000
Electric lighting	4,000
Grading	10,000
Total	158,500
Contingencies	8,000
Grand total	166,500

NOTE.—The following items are contained in a project now awaiting approval for construction from funds available until the passage of the pending House fortifications bill. The amendments submitted to the Senate subcommittee would extend the availability of these funds until June 30, 1921.

LUKE FIELD TECHNICAL BUILDINGS.

4 land plane hangars, 60 by 120, at $10,000	$40,000
For concrete foundations and floors for 5 additional hangars, and cost of their erection	22,350
1 garage (to house 50 vehicles composing: Motor cars, motor cycles, cargo, tank, photo, artillery, and machine shop trucks)	20,000
1 aero repair shop	30,000
1 motor repair shop, 65 by 128	25,000
1 miscellaneous repair shop, 30 by 90	5,000
3 storehouses, 30 by 125, at $10,000	30,000
Engineering	10,000
Retaining wall	25,000
Boathouse and docks	24,000
2 balloon hangars, Fort Ruger, at $12,000	24,000
Total	255,350

RECAPITULATION.

HAWAIIAN PROJECT—SENATE REVISION.

Luke Field	$819,374.00
Fort Kamehameha	314,126.00
Fort Ruger	166,500.00
Luke Field Technical Buildings	255,350.00
Contingencies	15,968.96
Total	1,571,318.96
Obligated for equipment since free balance reported to House Subcommittee	30,727.93
Grand total project	1,602,046.89
House bill appropriation	1,300,000.00
Funds requested continued by elimination of item covering same into Treasury on passage of bill	302,046.89
Grand total	1,602,046.89

Gen. MENOHER. There is one other short amendment, simply to complete the record, that is, a revocation of the provision for striking out that $302,000 for Oahu, simply to complete the record. Page 16, strike out lines 24 and 25.

Senator SMOOT. Is that all?

Gen. MENOHER. I believe so.

Thereupon, at 11.15 o'clock a. m., the subcommittee adjourned.

INDEX.

Lightning Source UK Ltd.
Milton Keynes UK
UKHW020724191218
334233UK00006B/90/P